W9-BVP-916

Laughter
in the Wilderness

LAUGHTER
IN THE WILDERNESS

Early American Humor to 1783

Edited
with an introduction by

W. Howland Kenney

KENT STATE UNIVERSITY PRESS

Library of Congress Cataloging in Publication Data

Main entry under Title:

Laughter in the Wilderness

  Bibliography: p.

  1. American literature—Colonial period, ca. 1600–1775. 2. American wit and humor.

I. Kenney, William Howland. PS530. L35 817'.1'08 75-44710

ISBN 0-87338-185-8

For Françoise

Table of Contents

[vii]

Acknowledgements

It is a great pleasure to acknowledge the encouragement and assistance of those several individuals who contributed to this edition. Paul Rohmann, director of the Kent State University Press, first suggested such a project to me and has offered valuable comments along the way. Judith Layng of the Music Department at Hiram College alerted me to Robert Hunter's *Androboros*, without which this collection would be much poorer. The jazz clarinetist and literary scholar Todd Roberts directed me to Nathaniel Hawthorne for insights into Puritan laughter. Edward Cohen of Rollins College very kindly allowed me to read the galleys of his insightful chapter on Ebenezer Cook's *The Sotweed Factor*. Catherine Hoffmann took time out from her writing and painting to offer me much needed encouragement. Monsieur Pierre Massardier never grumbled about the many inconveniences which attended my revisions of this manuscript in his home in Vesoul. Most of all, Françoise Marie Massardier has brought indispensible courage, wit, and loveliness both to this book and my life. We share many a good laugh in the wilderness. Any mistakes which may have crept into this effort are no laughing matter, however, and I take full responsibility for them.

PART ONE

Introduction

INTRODUCTION

There is an elusive, quicksilver quality about humor which defies the orderly classifications imposed by specialists. Indeed, the more one analyses, catalogues, and labels it, the more one destroys the spontaneity, surprise, and incredulity which produces laughter. As Max Eastman put it with telling irony:

> I must warn you reader, that it is not the purpose of this book to make you laugh. As you know, nothing kills the laugh quicker than to explain a joke. I intend to explain all jokes, and the proper and logical outcome will be, not only that you will not laugh now, but that you will never laugh again. So prepare for the descending gloom.[1]

In order to avoid plunging the reader into a black depression, while simultaneously preserving some early American laughter, the following introduction and readings attempt to locate and help us appreciate our earliest comic writers. In recognizing and enjoying the humor in our history, the past may not only inform but also enliven the present. If there is such a thing as "The General Reader," this book is his or hers and the specialists are invited to make use of it as they will.

In the creative leap of imagination which allows us to combine what is past into our present, the forests of America east of the Appalachian Mountains ring with the sounds of axes and musket fire. The villages carved out of the wilderness resound with the words of Christian piety which ordered and tamed it. Those interested enough to try can summon a living image of colonial life, but the sense of humor is missing.

1. Max Eastman, *Enjoyment of Laughter* (New York: Simon & Schuster, 1936), p. xv.

The settlers of the colonies are imagined to have been a pretty humorless band. Due to an overemphasis on the New England Puritans, as well as other factors, the seventeenth-century settlers seem remarkably dour. Their skies were filled with the smell of brimstone, codfish, and tobacco: their minds with the Protestant ethic. Whenever the idea of levity arises, it is generally agreed that early humor was "invented" by Benjamin Franklin.[2]

Of course, the colonists are often found to be very quaint. Trivial anecdotes culled from their writings allow us a benevolent chuckle or two.[3] Anthologies of our early literature and surveys of "American Humor" manage an occasional citation of Boston Magistrate Samuel Sewall's persistently unsuccessful courtings of assorted widows and sometimes a glimpse of William Byrd's lustings at Westover and in London.[4] Actually, however, neither Sewall nor Byrd reported on such matters for purposes of amusement and neither man wrote of them for a reading public. We are left, therefore, somewhere between a snicker and a sneer.

The nature of the questions, posed by those who have presented history to us, has contributed to assumptions of colonial gloom. One always writes or reads about the past with a strong sense of what was and is important. Until quite recently "history" has been thought to be the weighty recording of thundering armies, godly and not so godly statesmen, and social, economic, and political issues of a revealing, but certainly never humorous nature. In the process, certain aspects of the human experience come to be more important than others and matters of wit, whimsey, and laughter have been relegated to obscurity.

2. This is the impression left by such anthologies as Kenneth S. Lynn, ed., *The Comic Tradition in America* (New York: Norton Library, 1968), p. xiii, which states that "No pre-Revolutionary writer—except Franklin—had fully realized what sort of comic concoction might be brewed out of the roots of folk humor. . . ."

3. *William and Mary Quarterly,* 3d series, "Trivia."

4. Louis B. Wright, "Human Comedy in Early America," in Louis D. Rubin, ed., *The Comic Imagination in American Literature* (New Brunswick: Rutgers University Press, 1973), pp. 17–31. One outstanding exception to the rule is found in Brom Weber's fine anthology which, while suffering from the usual tendency to include colonial humor only as a short prelude to a much richer national humor, still presents many fine, and usually ignored, examples of colonial wit. Brom Weber, ed., *An Anthology of American Humor* (New York: Thomas Y. Crowell, 1962), pp. 1–127.

For a variety of reasons, among them the alternating pomposity, superficiality, and boredom of some bicentennial efforts, the loss of historical laughter is unfortunate. Humor is an unpretentious but very human trait which often requires great courage and strength. The comic insists on telling the whole truth when the pretenders to majesty, power, and control are imposing their various systems and definitions of life. One cannot quite grasp American history as a continuing reality until one poses the question "did they never laugh?"

The humorous pieces presented here should help to revise the idea that British colonists in North America were humoristically primitive. According to one scholar, " . . . the early settlers were a serious people struggling to establish themselves in a wilderness and they had little time for polite letters or for a literature of sheer entertainment."[5] In this view, life in the provinces was an endless round of toil, danger, and pious prayers, until, at some unspecified point in time, a sufficient level of material and social security freed men like Benjamin Franklin to cultivate impractical things like humor.

This approach has obscured the fact that wit and the comic spirit are often more functional than peripheral to human existence. According to one of the most perceptive and humane analysts, humor and joking ". . . make possible the satisfaction of an instinct . . . in the face of an obstacle which stands in its way. They circumvent this obstacle and in that way draw pleasure from a source which the obstacle had made inaccessible."[6] Thus, it is logical to argue that the very difficulties of wilderness life may have made a sense of humor just that much more important. Leaving family and friends in England, hazarding the dangerous voyage across the Atlantic, and braving the rigors of clearing "a hideous and desolate wilderness, full of wild beasts and wild men"[7] pro-

---

5. Wright, "Human Comedy," in Rubin, ed., *Comic Imagination,* p. 17.

6. Sigmund Freud, *Jokes and their Relation to the Unconscious,* ed. and trans. James Strachey (New York: Norton Library, 1963), pp. 101–03.

7. William Bradford, *Of Plymouth Plantation 1620–1647,* Samuel Eliot Morison, ed. (New York: Alfred A. Knopf, 1963), p. 62.

[5]

vided plenty of obstacles. Some surmounted them with grim determination, others with laughter.

An even more damaging interpretation has stipulated that colonial life remained culturally primitive after it became materially sophisticated. According to this reasoning, settlers could only echo British humor because they were so provincial. As one specialist has put it emphatically, "The fact is that our initial excursions into humor were largely weak and immature . . . indecisive and confused, highly derivative and labored, severely topical, and otherwise inexpert."[8] This thesis rests heavily on the writings of Benjamin Franklin who did "borrow" from such European humorists as Jonathan Swift, Addison and Steele, Rabelais, and La Rochefoucauld.[9] Since Franklin has been the focus of most discussions of early American humor, little doubt remained that those of comic inclinations stayed home when the New World was settled, or else did not publish.

There is a grain of truth in all this. Franklin borrowed, and some of our lesser known humorists like George Alsop and Ebenezer Cook returned to England, while Nathaniel Ward wrote for foreign audiences. Obviously, colonists had to clear fields and build houses and that kind of work is not necessarily conducive to jocularity. One supposes that snappy one-liners would have made little impression on such righteously resentful Native Americans as Metacom or Opechancanough. Nor would one expect a society which was clearing the wilderness to produce a clutch of courtly, snuff-taking wits. Pre-revolutionary America was in a position to cultivate more corn than courtliness, and it is unfair to expect many full-time satirists to emerge in its literature.

Humor, nevertheless, is a product of other things than nationality, cultural sophistication, or material security, although all those things play a role in shaping it. Moreover, it limits the subject too severely to treat only those people in America who spent their lives being witty or satiric. Humor is one part of the complex process of

8. Jesse Bier, *The Rise and Fall of American Humor* (New York: Holt, Rinehart & Winston, 1968), p. 32.

9. Theodore Hornberger, *Benjamin Franklin* (Minneapolis, Minn.: Univ. of Minnesota Press, 1962), pp. 15, 22, 24.

human perception and we can expect to encounter it in all societies even if only some of them can afford to produce specialists. In some instances, colonial humor was quite consciously refined, structured, and sophisticated. In others, it was just one facet of a broader set of reaction to the historic process of European migration westward. Both types of laughter are revealing in their own ways.

The comic imagination creates counterimages of human situations, fashioning enjoyment in the playful rearrangement of perceptions. When employed by the colonists of North America, humor helped define the experience of transplanting tradition to the western hemisphere. In creating a literature of humor, the colonists incorporated their outer experience into their perceptions of themselves. In reaching for the comic effect they consciously manipulated the major ingredients of wilderness life. We understand the past all the more for sharing their laughter.

A reading of early American humor reveals a quite uneven geographical distribution of comic writing. In a limited way, the old stereotype of the grimly scowling Puritan has some validity, at least in the sense that a much richer and more consistent humorous tradition emerged very early in the colonies to the south of New England. We will never know much of anything about such orally transmitted humor as circulated among the New Englanders, but their published works show them ill at ease with the power of laughter.

Puritans laughed, but their faith severely limited the range and intensity of their public and printed wit. As adherents to the doctrine of arbitrary election, Puritans assumed that God was omnipotent and man the object of a divinely-controlled drama more often tragic than comic in nature. Their belief in the efficacy of good works as a possible sign of election prevented them from finding the human situation "absurd." Man's foolishness was apparent, but brought to Puritans an "awareness that ultimate meaning belongs to God."[10]

10. Richard Boyd Hauck, *A Cheerful Nihilism: Confidence and 'The Absurd' in American Humorous Fiction* (Bloomington: Indiana University Press, 1971), pp. 19–20.

What this meant was that what non-Puritans might interpret as ridiculous, silly, grotesque, or comical, Puritans found deadly serious. Stumbling over a rock and landing on one's nose was more likely to be seen as a possible sign of divine displeasure than human comedy. So too, one could not find irony in man's struggle with environmental, biological, and social forces because that fated effort was a test of true faith. To laugh was to skirt the profane: either because one would mock the eternal drama of sin and redemption, or because laughter diverted one's attention from the need to transcend inherited sin. It was no matter of oversight that the word "humor" never appears in the indices to Perry Miller's works on New England Puritanism.[11] As one spokesman for the British Reformation put it:

Seeing the chief end of all religion is to redeem men from the spirit and vain conversation of this world, and to lead into inward communion with God, before whom if we fear always we are accounted happy; therefore, all the vain customs and habits thereof, both in word and deed, are to be rejected and forsaken by those who come to this fear; . . . as also the unprofitable plays, frivolous recreations, sportings, and gamings, which . . . divert the mind from the witness of God in the heart. . . .[12]

As a result of such attitudes, the government of the Bay Colony legislated against any public displays of humor which were ribald, satiric of the godly, or in any way profane. As late as 1712, the legislature responded to an apparent growth of secular humor in "An Act Against Intemperence, Immorality, and Profaneness, and for Reformation of Manners."[13]

And whereas evil communication, wicked, profane, filthy and obscene

11. Perhaps due to the latter, several pieces of Puritan wit were included in Miller and Thomas H. Johnson, eds., *The Puritans* (New York: The American Book Company, 1938), but the subject is not raised in *The New England Mind: The Seventeenth Century* (Cambridge: Harvard University Press, 1963) or in *The New England Mind From Colony to Province* (Cambridge: Harvard University Press, 1962).

12. Robert Barclay, as quoted in M. Conrad Hyers, ed., *Holy Laughter: Essays on Religion in the Comic Perspective* (New York: Seabury Press, 1969), p. 252.

13. *Ancient Charter, Colony, and Province Laws of Massachusetts Bay* (Boston, 1814). Cf. Colony Laws: ch. LI, sects. 7,8.

songs, composures, writings or prints, do corrupt the mind, and are incentives to all manner of impieties and debaucheries, more especially when digested, composed or uttered in imitation or mockery of devotion or religious exercises . . . whosoever shall be convicted of writing, printing, publishing of any filthy, obscene, or profane song, pamphlet, libel or mock sermon, in imitation or in mimicking of preaching, or any other part of divine worship . . . shall be punished by fine . . . not exceeding twenty pounds, or by standing on the pillory once or oftener, with an inscription of his crime in capital letters affixed over his head . . . .

This was merely an official expression of the long-standing Puritan effort to bring moral meaning to all human activity—an effort which brought the expulsion of Thomas Morton from America and continued with various "blue" laws regulating entertainments.

The kind of dangers inherent in laughter, the very unorthodox and even rebellious ingredients to which it can lend itself, is represented here in Thomas Morton's account of his censored activities at *Ma-re Mount*. The short portion included makes it clear that the early Separatists feared not merely humor's profanation of the holy, but also its power to reduce the saints to ridiculous proportions. Morton brought decadence and humorous sophistication, as well as rum and guns, into a new world which the Pilgrims were determined to reform, and for doing so he was summarily and even brutally expelled.

In spite of this stern warning, it was not quite the case that New England Puritanism was "the haunting fear that someone, somewhere, may be happy."[14] Puritans were flesh and blood and rested from their godly labor over beer, cider, and a moderate portion of rum. They also laughed, even in public, but in certain strictly stylized ways.

A reading of the permissible Puritan witticisms here included serves to confirm what Nathaniel Hawthorne suggested in his short story "My Kinsman Major Molineux."[15] In that story, Robin, a

14. H. L. Mencken, *A Mencken Chrestomathy* (New York: Alfred A. Knopf, 1967), p. 624.
15. Nathaniel Hawthorne, *The Snow-Image and Other Twice-Told Tales* (Boston: Houghton, Mifflin & Company, 1903), pp. 293–326.

poor but industrious farm boy, comes to Boston looking for his cousin. His father, a poor country minister, has only this wealthy connection, his brother's son Major Molineux, to offer Robin as patrimony. With his cousin as a patron, Robin hopes that he will find the help he needs to build a secure future.

In his fruitless searching, Robin becomes the butt of a secret joke: the town plans to tar-and-feather his kinsman that night, and for unspecified reasons. Soon the laughing and shouting procession barges its way to the church where Robin has been told he will see his relative. Tormenting, destructive, and "hellish" mirth sweeps before our eyes, as the townfolk parade the "majestic," "strong," "steady," wealthy, and famous Molineux before the roaring scorn of the people. Whatever the cause of this public display of laughter, and many feel that it describes the Revolutionary era, Hawthorne directs attention to its venomous and terrifying qualities and to its shared, communal function, as Robin himself joins the cruel hilarity.

This might be only the attack of one ideologue of the nineteenth century upon the actions of an earlier eighteenth-century culture, but it touches to the core of the pieces of earlier Puritan humor presented here. Nathaniel Ward, "The Simple Cobler of Aggawam in America," uses wit to solidify early Massachusetts communal solidarity and confidence by ridiculing the notions of religious toleration then gaining power in England and in the West Indies.[16] According to Ward, God himself laughed to see such misguided efforts at governmental restraint. Since Ward was so sure that toleration stemmed from inner doubt about the one, true faith, he further assured us that Jehovah "hath them in Derision."[17]

So too, after a thinly veiled apology for the lightness of his tone, Ward hurls some painfully sharp verbal darts at the vanity and folly of contemporary females who, in Ward's opinion, ran an increasingly frenzied fashion race. Ward "parrotizes" the gaudy in the name of the godly, and such laughter as emerges results from

16. Robert D. Arner, "The Simple Cobler of Aggawam: Nathaniel Ward and the Rhetoric of Satire," *Early American Literature*, V, 3 (Winter 1970–71), 3–16.

17. Ward's inspiration was biblical. Psalms 2:2 finds the Lord laughing derisively at the misguided, empty ambitions of earthly rulers.

ridicule, scorn, and invective. Humor becomes a pillory which shames and embarrasses in the name of reformation. Pushing the comic technique of exaggeration to its limits, Ward inflates small details of attire into such monstrous deformities that one laughs at the prospect of outlandish pretension. Having been seduced into appreciation of his images and linguistic creations, the reader's laughter, in itself, demonstrates the author's point.

A quite similar effect is produced by *New England's Annoyances*. Upon commencing the ballad, one is amused by the recitation of vexations endured by this hardy band of long-suffering countrymen. By the time one has come to empathize with their smiling resignation, it is almost impossible to shun the concluding sneer at the "scum" who doubted the ultimate value of the New England Way.

This same use of humor in the name of social control is a thread which runs through and gives meaning to the travel journal of Mrs. Sarah Kemble Knight. Moreover, as this often-frightened, but courageous lady made her way through the New England wilderness to New York City, she unavoidably encountered non-Puritan settlers. In the process, Mrs. Knight sharpened her tongue on the whole gamut of influences and people alien to her own way of life. Wherever encountered, be they blacks, Indians, Quakers, Frenchmen, barflies, or country-bumpkins, this tart-tongued pilgrim rallied her spirits by making them all the butts of her jokes. In this way, she was able to take her sanctity into the lair of the Antichrist. Peeking out, rather reluctantly, to see how it went with the rest of the world, Sarah Kemble Knight could assure herself that it went on around her but not nearly so well as in Boston.

Whether due to the passage of time or a less pretentious motive, Mrs. Knight's journal is much funnier to us than the Wardian wit. When the two are placed beside the fragments of New England balladry, it seems clear that even the earliest and most zealous Puritans laughed. Their laughter was more likely to stem from caustic ridicule of anyone beyond their borders. Given their piety, Puritans did not approve of ribaldry and burlesque, but they obviously enjoyed witticisms and a dry, caustic sarcasm.

[11]

Ward's performance surely qualifies as wilderness laughter regardless of its lack of the broad generosity associated with current attitudes toward "humor." In any event, when Puritans laughed, they did so for reasons which others shared: laughter helped them order their world and protect their identity.

There is a noticeable change in New England humor by the middle of the eighteenth-century. Joseph Green's *Entertainment for a Winter's Evening* is remarkable for the degree to which it presents a modified social and cultural role for humor in New England. Not only is this a celebration of secularism and "the bottle and bowl," but the laughter stems from Green's easy toleration of human self-indulgence in an overtly religious context. The jolly Masons go through the motions of orthodoxy comforted by a sly wink from their loyal brother in the pulpit. The reader was helped to identify the individuals involved and applaud their noisy parade from bar-room to church and back again. It is hard to imagine Nathaniel Ward indulging such low burlesque of lofty ideals, and Green's popular pamphlet marks the vast changes which time brought to the New England mind. As such, Green's *Entertainment* provides a bridge from the early Puritan didactic wit to the far more earthy and secular humor produced much earlier in the Southern colonies.

The comic tradition in New England is recovered in bits and pieces, pulled, as it were, from behind the heavy curtain of sober orthodoxy. The sound of Southern jocularity leaps quickly and directly through time, providing a deep and consistent interpretation of life in the wilderness. George Alsop, nearly one hundred years before Joseph Green, penned a wild and irreverent portrait of colonial Maryland which marked a strong start of the "Cavalier" ethos in America. At first glance it appears that Alsop and his appreciative audience were guilty of exactly what Nathaniel Ward would have charged: the profanation of the holy and the reduction of man to a grunting, wallowing, and craven beast. Alsop laughingly labeled his book "a bastard brat" conceived in a perverse tryst between the author and the god of youth, travel, and colonies. Even the ever-so-slightly wayward Sarah Knight would have declared Alsop a devilish fiend of nihilistic chaos.

[12]

Alsop could not have cared less about such "constipated" views but the two were not entirely without common ground. George Alsop played the court jester for his revered Cecilius Calvert, Lord Baltimore of Maryland. As such, a consistent strain, not uncongenial to Knight, runs through all the silly antics and anal-oral indulgences. Like Madam Knight and the Simple Cobler of Aggawam, Alsop was not about to let the Maryland wilderness engulf his "Civilized" sensibilities. Willing to be far more tolerant of the provincial bumpkins and "absurd" Indians he found, Alsop was no more able to identify with them than Mrs. Knight was with "Bumkin Simpers" and "Jone Tawdry." Humor, and in this case wit, firmly identified the humorist as a mannered gentleperson among the savages. In adding the sum of his sexual asides, double-entendres, outrageous punning, twisted historical allusions, and playful figures of speech, Alsop tried to be a seventeenth-century "Gentleman Adventurer," who, like Captain John Smith, was so exceedingly intrepid that the wilderness world provided him just another diverting playground. Greatness of spirit among those "of the better-sort" could take something like America in stride. What Knight and Ward destroyed with their blistering sarcasm, Alsop transformed with the laughing denial that it was really a "serious" matter.

Alsop presents a minor dilemma: he spent only four years in Maryland and published his book in England. Moreover, it is clear that he, like Ward and Cook, wrote primarily for English readers. To a degree, therefore, our early humor was not so much American as British. This may disappoint those in search of "American Humor" but need not concern those who are looking for humor in the prenational years of North America. We are, after all, dealing with people settled in Britain's colonies. There was no printing press in Maryland before 1685, and none in Virginia until 1730.[18] Where else but in London was Alsop to publish? Furthermore, Alsop used America as his comic device, thereby opening to the

18. See Lawrence C. Wroth, *The Colonial Printer* (Portland: The Southworth-Anthoensen Press, 1938), ch. 2.

[13]

imagination an entirely new set of satiric possibilities which would later be seen as typical of American humor.

One parallel characteristic of our early humor is the way in which it reflects movement and impermanence. Alsop, for example, satirized the entire transatlantic process as would befit the comically inclined migrant. His barbs were aimed at England, at Maryland, and at the ocean voyage. Mrs. Knight used her journey as her major comic source. Ward spoke of the West Indies, England, and New England. The result is not identifiably or uniquely American but reflective of colonial realities. This is fitting and should not be dismissed as a primitive prelude to something that came after.

Despite theories about cultural primitivism before Benjamin Franklin, *The Sotweed Factor* by Ebenezer Cook stands alongside the best of American humorous writing. Indeed, Cook's satiric skill and his candid revelation of the absurdness of early British Maryland deserve great attention in their own right, although their spirit has been well served in John Barth's novel of nearly the same name.[19] The poem is the only thoroughly comic treatment of early America, and, as such, it is presented in its entirety.

A reading of Alsop's Maryland and Knight's New England should make clear that Cook's materials were not altogether original, for the same themes appear less fully developed elsewhere. *Bumpkin Simpers* and *Jone Tawdry*, for example, would have fit nicely into Cook's poetic drama, but unlike the humorists who preceded him, Cook brought such characters very close to a venally democratic triumph over effete European pretensions. In much the same way, Alsop's warnings about the crafty Maryland sodbusters served to caution his gentlemanly readers. In *The Sotweed Factor,* British confidence and culture have been completely undone by New World life. The swaggering merchant is stripped of his clothes, his wares, his dignity, and finally his very sanity, as the raucous revels of American confusion beat a roaring guffaw around his ears. The foppish tobacco merchant is left to

19. *The Sot-Weed Factor* (New York: Grosset & Dunlap, 1966).

[14]

utter unheard and ineffective curses upon a world too chaotic and self-indulgent to bother listening to them.

In another sense, it is quite fitting that much of early American humor was printed outside of North America. Ward, Alsop, and Cook used the New World as a device for satirizing the Old World; Ward used the stricter piety of a provincial shoemaker as a foil for English decadence, while Alsop drew comic contrasts between Maryland and "home." Cook's antihero provided a good American laugh on British pretensions but also turned the laughter against the rudeness and corruption of provincial realities. Since *The Sotweed Factor* stopped short of naming the names of those who sullied American innocence, Britons could enjoy laughing at such distant antics. When a printing press was established in Maryland, Cook's poem was quickly published here, but its bitter concluding curse was discreetly modified.

Had Alsop or Cook allowed their satiric gifts freedom enough to fasten upon well-known officials, it is much less likely that their efforts ever would have seen print. Radical humor, the savage, caustic, wild, and irreverent barbs which attack the throat of official absurdities, were quite likely whispered about the colonies but firmly suppressed in public through the universal system of governmental licensing and censorship of the press.

Throughout the colonies, the press was not assumed to be a free organ of popular expression but rather an arm of official orthodoxy. Here it need only be mentioned that James Franklin and John Peter Zenger, in Boston and New York respectively, encountered stiff governmental penalties for using humor against officialdom: Franklin merely for hinting comically that Massachusetts was going less than all out in suppressing pirates, and Zenger for printing anti-authoritarian stories about the governor.[20] That their humor might point to realities was considered no justification, but treason. It was this official policy in a hierarchical colonial world which explains why most early American irreverence was not

20. Leonard W. Levy, *Legacy of Suppression: Freedom of Speech and Press in Early America* (Cambridge: Harvard University Press, 1960), ch. 4.

printed here. In the highly personal politics of the British empire, the revolutionary spirit of spontaneous satire was a dangerous weapon which might just as easily be turned against its wielder.

This political context illuminates the witty observations of William Byrd, II. To record and lighten the job of locating a Virginia-North Carolina borderline, Byrd kept a journal of the expedition which saw only private circulation among Byrd's friends while the author lived. So harsh were his satiric attacks upon North Carolinians, and even one well-known member of the Virginia delegation, that publication would have embroiled him in some nasty political wrangles. The mature sense of the decorous discretion expected of a Virginia planter-statesman led Byrd to a private circulation of his manuscript.

Moreover, even when the objects of his ridicule were long dead, the manuscript was found morally offensive.[21] Earthy joking and laughter, pointed at the gap between public morality and private reality, remained radical long after Zenger had won his court fight against government censorship of the press. Even after political satire found acceptance, the press was expected to preserve public decorum, be that nicely dictated by religious orthodoxy or secular propriety. Byrd's little poem and major portions of his diaries remain to this day something of an embarrassment.

Quite beyond any questions of politics and censorship the role of the Southern gentleman planter encouraged a refined, haughty, and biting sense of humor. At its best, this social role produced men who embellished their ample leisure time through the cultivation of arts and letters. A sense of humor was an important mark of one's contented detachment from the drearier aspects of common toil and it provided a useful mark of social distinction. It would never do to share the heavy raucity of common farmers, and a cold indifference provided a firm barrier between the tavern tables. The provincial Southern gentleman took his leisure with his peers and only among them did he exchange anecdotes and witticisms. In these moments,

21. Louis B. Wright, ed., *The Prose Works of William Byrd of Westover: Narratives of a Colonial Virginian* (Cambridge: Harvard University Press, 1966), pp. 1–3, 22.

[16]

humor evinced one's sophistication, learning, and awareness of nuance.

It was within this context that William Byrd wrote and circulated his *History of the Dividing Line* and substantially the same milieu stimulated and appreciated Dr. Alexander Hamilton's *Itinerarium*. Hamilton was a founder of the Tuesday Club of Annapolis, Maryland, a group of convivial gentlemen who met regularly to satirize and parodize major issues and personalities of the day.[22] Hamilton wrote a three-volume history of the club which functioned as a natural and valued part of life among the "better-sort." It was a decidedly private organization which injected gaiety into the sleepy tedium of Maryland life.

In 1744, Dr. Hamilton temporarily abandoned his merry comrades to travel north into New York and New England. His journey provided ample occasions for the observation of human follies and a rich variety of colorful personalities. The *Itinerarium* which recorded Hamilton's impressions and reactions to the northern colonies is a striking example of the picaresque narrative previously used by Alsop, Cook, Knight, and William Byrd, and it is a shame that those intrepidly cheerful writers could not have compared stories with Hamilton over a potent bowl of punch in Annapolis. Together, these five colonial writers produced the single most consistent and revealing genre of early American humor. Beset on all sides by a crude, cruel, and vexing wilderness, Dr. Hamilton was able to find a satisfying and fortifying amusement which he happily recorded for posterity.

Just how important a sense of humor could be is further revealed by Governor Robert Hunter's *Androboros*.[23] In this mock-heroic play, which ridiculed Francis Nicholson, a seasoned royal official, and mocked the elected representatives of New York's settlers, Hunter reached for a larger reading public than most of the Southern humorists. Because he was governor, Hunter had access to the

22. Elaine G. Breslaw, "Wit, Whimsy, and Politics: The Uses of Satire by the Tuesday Club of Annapolis, 1744 to 1756," *William and Mary Quarterly*, 3d ser., XXXII, 2 (April 1975), 304.

23. Lawrence H. Leder, "Robert Hunter's ANDROBOROS," *Bulletin of the New York Public Library*, LXVIII (March 1964), 153–60.

[17]

press of William Bradford and used it for far more political purposes than any of his predecessors. In so doing, Robert Hunter initiated what would become a running humoristic debate—one which later royal officials ultimately lost.

Despite the elitist elements of Hunter's performance, it is not insignificant that this governor turned to burlesque and slapstick to elicit the good will of the literate electorate. Those whom he mocked had bedeviled him so effectively that laughter was called upon to provide some common ground and good will. One of laughter's gifts is its ability to "adjust 'incompatible standards without resolving the clash between them, . . .' "[24] Hunter, for all his denigration of the *demos*, was using wit to tame democratic forces beyond the reach of his practical control.

Governor Hunter's comic attack upon the stubbornly independent New York assembly was an affirmation of gentlemanly civility in a wilderness full of ignorance and pretension, but it raised the likelihood of an emerging popular humor stemming from less socially exalted sources. Of all the ways of appealing to the public, Hunter chose comedy, and a reading of the colonial newspapers reveals that many an obscure provincial was turning to satiric writing, long the preserve of the social elite. Ever so gradually, humor became less aristocratic and more bourgeois, and the Hunters of provincial letters were put on the defensive.

The colonial newspapers, for all their frequent efforts to mime the aristocratic pretensions of a Robert Hunter, were produced by and for the bourgeoisie. Printed in the several older, coastal cities in British America, they were nearly the sole means by which artisans, professional men, and merchants could inform themselves of European events, transatlantic shipping patterns, and the exchange of goods. In the American scramble for wealth and preferment, the newspapers were valuable tools and the humorous pieces which appeared in them reflected the ambitions of an American middle-class eager to prove literary sophistication.

Two qualities which run through colonial newspaper humor are a tendency to fasten upon sexual subjects and, secondly, to treat

24. Wylie Sypher, as quoted by Breslaw, *William and Mary Quarterly*, 304.

[18]

them in a voyeuristic fashion. Zenger's New York *Weekly Journal* peeked into the racy highjinks of the *Hunc Ober Dees* providing not only the information that such immoral things were going on, but also a titter and giggle that it went on in private, clandestine moments in defiance of accepted morality. The reader's laughter was directed away from himself and onto the abstracted chasm between moral pretensions and social behavior.

An unexpectedly common characteristic of newspaper wit is its preoccupation with the "warfare between the sexes." Again and again, newspapers carried reports of anonymous but storied womanizers who were publicly beset by a pride of revenge-minded victims and soundly beaten and humiliated for their transgressions. Whether or not these were reports of actual events, the reader could laugh at the well-deserved comeuppance while savoring a private satisfaction that the irate females openly admitted their past follies in their public exorcism. The state no longer placed either malefactor or victim in the stocks but newspapers stories provided a public pillory of didactic laughter.

It is this recurrent impulse to communicate some moral lesson which helped to determine whether or not a piece of humor reached print. George Alsop's burlesque, Cook's scathing denunciation of Maryland, and Byrd's ribaldry affirmed nothing so much as the endurance of the individual over political and governmental absurdities. This was not the lesson which our colonial governments saw fit to propagate. In the case of William Byrd, it was one thing to poke fun at the Anglican chaplain in the privacy of the wilderness, but quite another to publish it. The "better-sort" understood this distinction.

The political requirements and moral imperatives of early American printing made satire a particularly popular genre for public humor. From the time of Juvenal's *Satires* in Roman literature, satire was a means of criticizing and censuring some prevailing vice or folly. The satirist used exaggeration and the juxtaposition of ideals and realities to stimulate reform. The writer of satire could thus present himself as a bastion of social and cultural purity and his humor as an instrument for social ordering.

[19]

This was the perfect pose for the would-be satirist in a conservative culture. Ward, Alsop, Cook, and a brace of newspaper printers could give full rein to their comic fancies so long as the satiric form was maintained as the structuring device, and only if the satire was not aimed at the government.

This same situation encouraged the use of the satiric *persona* or *mask* with which the author could obscure his real identity, thus avoiding reprisals, and pose as an anonymous "friend of virtue" or guardian of tradition. The satiric persona had a long tradition in English literature and was readily adopted by such humorists as Nathaniel Ward who called himself, fittingly, *Theodore de la Guard*.

The provincial newspapers and magazines contain many essays, poems, and anecdotes which were intended to be humorous, I am sure. Most of them miss the mark now, as I believe they did then and they have not been included. Most were heavily dependent upon English models and strove mightily to be "just terribly" sophisticated. The major device usually took the form of an indolent cafe wit, so freed from labor that his time could be occupied in satirizing the manners of society. Women's fashions were a favorite source of satiric pleasure and most of the humor was sadly humorless. Despite their meager achievement, such efforts indicate how important it was for a certain type of colonist to transcend the crass world of the wilderness and enter the urban stream of Addisonian wit.

From the wide variety of supposedly comic efforts printed in the newspapers, it is evident that Benjamin Franklin was part of a broader, if minor, cultural movement toward urban wit and sophistication. The same proliferation of journalistic humor leaves little doubt that Franklin was the most effective devotee of the comic muse. Many another anonymous writer strove to satirize the hypocrisies of colonial urban life, using the familiar devices of the masked persona, mock-epic style, and the fanciful fabrication of "historical" events. None of them did those things nearly as well as Franklin.

At the same time, when Franklin's comic pieces are put within the context of an entire colonial humorous tradition, the limitations of his laughter are also apparent. Franklin was the best of one type of humorist: those who followed the paths of Addison, Steele, and Jonathan Swift in satirizing urban life. Here, Franklin cleverly reworked existing models, finding convincing colonial counterparts for European situations and character types. Within his chosen structures, Benjamin Franklin paid keen attention to nuance, pun, double-entendre, and a rich vein of linguistic wit fashioned from the sly juxtaposition of incongruous words and images.

What Franklin chose not to do was to work with the more obvious American comic themes so wonderfully employed by Alsop, Cook, Byrd and Hamilton. Perhaps because he had dedicated himself to creating a more perfect and rational modern society, Franklin drew very little upon the themes of travel, wilderness confusion, or Native American life. One will look in vain for frontiersmen, fur-traders, Indians, and even common farmers in his comic essays. Instead, Franklin worked in a humorous world of artisans, tavern-keepers, and ambitious tradesmen. His was a thoroughly urban, bourgeois milieu and Franklin probably took pleasure in the difficulty of identifying the exact locale. The more it appeared to be a major western city, the better.

The precise sort of comedy which Franklin ignored is found in two dialect letters which were written in mid-century Virginia. The exact authorship of these satisfying creations is not certain, but they emerged from a group of representatives in the House of Burgesses who used satire to mock the pretensions and blunders of royal governor Dinwiddie.[25] Probably the work of John Mercer of Marlborough, they were the kind of satires written by the "Hiccory Hill Club," a group of literate colonials who patterned their efforts after the "Tuesday Club" in Annapolis, Maryland.

In these literary gatherings, leaders of the colonial assemblies produced mock debates and satiric essays about their political

25. Richard Beale Davis, "The Colonial Virginia Satirist," *Transactions of the American Philosophical Society,* 57, pt. 1 (Phila.: American Philosophical Society, 1967), pp. 5–18.

[21]

struggles with royal authorities. At mid-century, these conflicts were exaggerated by the French-and-Indian War but had not as yet reached irreconcilable proportions. Consequently, laughter provided the illusion of resolution and the cement of compromise.

In form and substance the dialect letters point to future patterns of American humor. Earlier satirists had mocked the ignorant provincials, even when they ruefully admitted their rugged sagacity. Here the tables have been turned and the tough, "savvy," and barely literate frontiersman has become the voice of wisdom and sanity. Governor Dinwiddie and his policies are gouged by the democratic dogs who had earlier cringed from their haughty masters. Constance Rourke has shown very clearly that the wilderness sage became a form of American self-congratulation in the early nineteenth century. Our collection should clarify how far back in the colonial past this comic mode originated.[26]

The American War for Independence stimulated a rash of rebellious satires of and by both sides in that struggle. Satire had been the primary vehicle for eighteenth-century provincial humorists and the revolution brought a proliferation of satiric forms rather than any major stylistic innovations. The Hudibrastic genre, employed by Ebenezer Cook at the beginning of the century, remained highly popular through the war years.[27] Satire, always a tool of conservative reformers, was aptly suited to an imperial crisis in which both sides claimed to be champions of order, sanity, and political purity.

The twenty years between the end of the French-and-Indian War and the conclusion of the struggle for independence intensified issues such as aristocracy versus democracy, learning and ignorance, and civilization versus savagery—issues treated by colonial humorists from the beginning. In a subtle but definite and important manner, revolutionary satirists departed from the past by openly employing humor as a weapon. Where Hunter, Hamilton

26. Constance Rourke, *American Humor: A Study of the National Character* (New York: Harcourt, Brace & Co., 1931), chs. 1–2.

27. Bruce Ingham Granger, *Political Satire in the American Revolution 1763–1783* (Ithaca: Cornell Univ. Press, 1960), pp. 6–8.

and other pre-revolutionary wits had used laughter to help balance contradictions, Philip Freneau, John Trumbull, Mercy Warren and others used their talents to resolve all contradictions by destroying the opposition.

As a result of this change in the context of humorous writing, satire became less indirect and more prone to invective and abuse. In the hands of patriots and tories alike, the metaphors and similes became more and more harsh, both sides imputing bestial, craven, and hypocritical behavior to the other. Satirists ranged over all facets of the crisis, but the military aspects of the war drew their heaviest fire. In the heat of battle humorous techniques were turned into arms of psychological warfare and although laughter was sought, the primary goal was its political effect.

Some of the patriot satirists produced works of wit which have been widely admired since. In an effort to preserve an accurate sense of revolutionary humor, without reproducing familiar works by the more famous writers such as Freneau, Trumbull, and Hopkinson, lesser-known, but representative selections of wartime wit conclude this collection. Each was presented anonymously at the time and an effort has been made to represent both sides while favoring the victors.

A reading of this collection may illustrate several things. In the first place, the comic imagination was not lacking in the colonies. It is true that the New England Puritans did not encourage it, but there has been a tendency to overemphasize their somber influences in what was a much larger American scene. Even among the Puritans, laughter arose from ironic witticisms and holy satire and was a valuable tool in building the city upon a hill. Within the confines of Puritan thought, the elect might enjoy a carefully masked, hidden laugh at the follies of others as they trod on determinedly to their reward.

Outside of New England, a grasp of the absurd and an ability to embrace human failings in therapeutic jocularity emerged very early. In the Southern colonies, George Alsop, Ebenezer Cook, William Byrd, and others created a rowdy, irreverent, and earthy humoristic literature which utilized the wilderness as a major

[23]

device. In Southern writing a vivid portrait of a uniquely American environment takes shape and one can trace several of the great themes of our history: utopian dreams in contact with brutal realities, aristocratic hauteur among the savage unwashed, and even the ability of British imperialism in dealing with an expanding frontier. These issues were far from resolved when our early humorists reflected upon them, and the ability to laugh about them made the ambiguities more acceptable.

The printed humor of the colonies was often indebted to English models. Humor had been the preserve of the "better-sort," and colonists made a conscious attempt to ape the great satirists of England and the continent. Samuel Butler, Jonathan Swift and the *Spectator* essays provided stylistic models for many provincial wits. When many of these writers turned to their own uniquely American environment for inspiration, however, they produced an original comic literature in spite of themselves. The dense and tangled forests, the exotic and frightening Indians, and the very process of building a society in such circumstances provided unprecedented comedic oppportunities. In grappling with such new themes, old forms and structures were transformed.

Among other facets of later "American" humor, the colonists developed the tall-tale about wilderness beasts and frontier courage as early as 1666 when George Alsop published his book on Maryland. The picaresque narrative of the comic pilgrim inevitably arose from colonial immigrant experience. So too, the rustic backwoodsman as satiric savant of the pretensions of urban civilization was used in the 1630s when Nathaniel Ward posed as the Simple Cobler. To a degree, the mere fact of being in America made everyone there a backwoods person in relation to the home country. Some rejected the reality by bringing civilized wit into play against the wilderness but in so doing only underlined the actual historical process. Benjamin Franklin used humor to promote urban sophistication when he lived in Philadelphia, but he thoroughly enjoyed playing the frontier sage when representing the colonists in Europe.

To an extent, laughter is often provoked by the incongruous

[24]

juxtaposition of opposites. A reading of colonial and revolutionary American humor illustrates how well suited the immigrant experience was to comic interpretation. Depending upon one's vision, the arrival of a haughty European in an uncharted wilderness could mark the triumph of civilization over savagery or a comic clashing of opposites. One could bemoan as vexing the encounters with unexpected and inexplicable situations, or one could laugh at the confusions and blunders which they produced. It all depended upon whether one emphasized the ultimate goal of settlement or incidents along the way.

Since the ocean voyage to America and the penetration of the tangled forests were heroic experiences, whether measured by the time, effort, or precedents involved, the colonial experience lent itself to burlesque. The interpretation of such an elevated, instructive, and dramatic subject in a trivial, earthy fashion developed rather automatically from the grim realities of day-to-day experience. Exchanging a boatload of woolens and cutlery for a cargo of smoking tobacco would have produced little laughter had it not been for the inflated and misguided expectations of one of the parties about the other. Struggling through the undergrowth on horseback would have been cause for cursing alone had the intrepid cavalier not worn his best velvet suit in expectation of finding a Garden of Eden. The administration of justice in itself was a sober subject, but when, in America, it took place in a pumpkin patch and involved three different languages or when the judge and attorneys were not only illiterate but drunk, then it was hard to avoid a comic interpretation.

In creating a humorous literature, British colonists in North America consciously manipulated the major ingredients of wilderness life. By looking carefully at those things which *they* found funny and by noticing how they produced humorous effects, one follows their progressive mastery over themselves and their environment. This is the important difference between laughing at their blunders in the comfort of retrospect, and sharing the fruits of their creative process, for it is only in the latter that we see their intellects at work. A creative humor can be consciously created only by

[25]

someone who possesses a clear and firm comprehension of what is going on around him. Madam Knight, George Alsop, Ebenezer Cook, Dr. Hamilton, Benjamin Franklin and the rest saw quite clearly both where they were and from whence they had come. That they found some aspects of their worlds laughable—and sometimes found the entire prospect absurd—marks their ability to detach themselves from the immediate and the apparent and carefully rearrange, in a playful manner, their own reactions, perceptions, and experiences. Given the hardships they surmounted, they often needed laughter. By producing it they evinced strength and clarity of vision.

Today, nearly two hundred years after the Declaration of American Independence and over three hundred years after George Alsop arrived in Maryland, we pause to celebrate whatever seems important to us about our past. One savours the occasion to follow those creative, perceptive souls who laughed in the face of their own wandering confusion. Perhaps something of their infectious bouyancy, their errant whimsies, and especially their jocular resilience will inform the present. The distant ring of their laughter will scarcely banish all existing gloom, but it just might create a small, unpretentious empathy and continuity.

W. Howland Kenney
Kent, Ohio
July 12, 1975

PART TWO

Humor and Holiness
in Early New England

THOMAS MORTON'S SATIRE

OF MILES STANDISH AND THE PILGRIMS

[1632]

THOMAS Morton is one of the more shadowy characters who moved into and out of the North American scene, leaving precious few personal records. He is thought to have been born around 1579 in the West Country of England and subsequently trained for the law at Clifford's Inn. Thereafter, almost nothing is known about Morton's life until he arrived in Massachusetts in the spring of 1624.[1] Morton established a fur-trading post at what was called Mount Wollaston, the present site of Quincy, Massachusetts. Morton's trading activities, his tolerant Anglicanism, and, of course, the May Day games and revels he indulged, brought efforts by the Plymouth Pilgrims to terminate his settlement. As Governor William Bradford put it,

> After this they fell to great licentiousness and led a dissolute life, pouring out themselves into all profaneness. And Morton became Lord of Misrule, and maintained (as it were) a School of Atheism. And after they had got some goods into their hands, and got much by trading with the Indians, they spent it as vainly in quaffing and drinking, both wine and strong waters in great excess (and, as some reported) £10 worth in a morning. They also set up a maypole, drinking and dancing about it many days together, inviting the Indian women for their consorts, dancing and frisking together like so many fairies, or furies, rather; and worse practices. As if they had anew revived and celebrated the feasts of the Roman goddess Flora, or the beastly practices of the mad Bacchanalians. Morton likewise, to show his poetry composed sundry rhymes and verses, some tending to lasciviousness, and others to the detraction and scandal of some persons, which he affixed to this idle or idol maypole.[2]

1. Donald F. Connors, *Thomas Morton* (New York: Twayne Publishers, 1969), p. 13.
2. *Of Plymouth Plantation 1620–1647 by William Bradford,* Samuel Eliot Morison, ed. (New York: Alfred A. Knopf, 1963), pp. 205–06.

The beleaguered Morton got some sweet revenge for his treatment by Bradford's men, who, led by Captain Miles Standish, marched on Merry Mount, captured Morton and prior to sending him back to England, exiled him to a barren island off the coast. The martyr to merriment wrote a satiric account of the affair, including Captain "Shrimp" (Standish). Entitled *New English Canaan; or New Canaan . . .,* Morton's version of the famous incidents has received much less attention than the official Bradford *History.* One reason for this is surely the decidedly "nonserious" tone of his rebuttal. If history is the story of the winners of past struggles, then mirth and jollity are dropped from our view of the past. Another small portion of our humorous tradition is hereby resurrected.

W.H.K.

OF THE REVELLS OF NEW CANAAN

The Inhabitants of Pasonagessit (having translated the name of their habitation from that ancient Salvage name to Ma-re Mount; and being resolved to have the new name confirmed for a memorial to after ages) did devise amongst themselves to have it performed in a solemne manner with Revels, & merriment after the old English custome: prepared to sett up a Maypole upon the festivall day of Philip and Jacob;[3] & therefore brewed a barrell of excellent beare, & provided a case of bottles to be spent, with other good cheare, for all commers of that day. And because they would have it in a compleat forme, they had prepared a song fitting to the time and present occasion. And upon May-day they brought the Maypole to the place appointed, with drumes, gunnes, pistols, and other fitting instruments, for that purpose; and there erected it with the help of Salvages, that came thether of purpose to see the manner of our Revels. A goodly pine tree of 80. foote longe, was reared up, with a peare of buckshorns nayled one, somewhat neare unto the top of it:

3. Thomas Morton, *New English Canaan; or New Canaan . . .,* (London, 1632), in Peter Force, ed., *Tracts and Other Papers . . . of the Colonies in North America,* II (Washington: P. Force, 1838), 89–96.

[30]

where it stood as a faire sea marke for directions; how to finde out
the way to mine Host of Ma-re Mount. . . .

There was likewise a merry song made, which (to make their
Revells more fashionable) was sung with a Corus, every man
bearing his part; which they performed in a daunce, hand in hand
about the Maypole, whiles one of the Company sung, and filled out
the good liquor. . . .

THE SONGE

Drinke and be merry, merry, merry boyes,
Let all your delight be in the Hymens joyes,
Jô to Hymen now the day is come,
About the merry Maypole take a Roome.
Make greene garlons, bring bottles out;
And fill sweet Nectar, freely about,
Uncover thy head, and feare no harme,
For hers good liquor to keepe it warme.
Then drinke and be merry, &c.
Jô to Hymen, &c.
Nectar is a thing assign'd,
By the Deities owne minde,
To cure the hart opprest with greife,
And of good liquors is the cheife,
Then drinke, &c.
Jô to Hymen, &c.
Give to the Mellancholly man,
A cup or two of't now and than;
This physick' will soone revive his bloud,
And make him be of a merrier moode.
Then drinke, &c.
Jô to Hymen, &c.
Give to the Nymphe thats free from scorne,
No Irish; stuff nor Scotch over worne,
Lasses in beaver coats come away,

[31]

Yee shall be welcome to us night and day.
To drinke and be merry, &c.
Jô to Hymen, &c.

This harmeless mirth made by younge men (that lived in hope to have wifes brought over to them, that would save them a laboure to make a voyage to fetch any over) was much distasted, of the precise Seperatists: that keepe much a doe, . . . troubling their braines more then reason would require about things that are indifferent . . . they set upon my honest host at a place, called Wessaguscus, where (by accident) they found him.

[Morton escaped his captors as they were sleeping off some celebration of their own.] The word which was given with an alarme, was, o he's gon, he's gon, what shall we doe he's gon? the rest (halfe a sleepe) start up in a maze, and like rames, ran their heads one at another full butt in the darke.

Thier grand leader Captaine Shrimp tooke on most furiously, and tore his clothes for anger, to see the empty nest, and their bird gone.

The rest were eager to have torne theire haire from theire heads, but it was so short, that it would give them no hold; Now Captaine Shrimp thought in the losse of this prize (which hee accoumpted his Master peece,) all his honor would be lost for ever. . . . Hee takes eight persons more to him, and (like the nine Worthies of New Canaan) they imbarque with preparation against Ma-re-Mount, where this Monster of a man (as theire phrase was) had his denne; the whole number, (had the rest not bin from home, being but seaven,) would have given Captaine Shrimpe (a quondam Drummer,) such a wellcome, as would have made him wish for a Drume as bigg as Diogenes tubb, that hee might have crept into it out of sight . . ., mine Host was content to yeelde . . . and did capitulate . . . Captain Shrimpe and the rest of the nine worthies, made themselves (by this outragious riot) Masters of mine Hoste of Ma-re Mount, and disposed of what hee had at his plantation.

[32]

EARLY NEW ENGLAND

BALLADS

The two ballads about life in New England are tantalizing. Both hint strongly about a level of folk humor which, due to its exclusively oral transmission, is largely lost to history. The vast proportion of early American humor which has survived was produced by an educated provincial elite who had access to the press and to those who controlled what it printed. Here, on the other hand, two tempting morsels of seventeenth-century New England popular thought invite us to step out of the meeting houses and into a far less intellectual and even more secular world.

It is interesting to note that neither of these ballads was originally published in New England. *New England's Annoyances* survived in manuscript and reached print only in this century. Although it is a song of regional loyalty, the only religious reference tends to treat Puritanism rather ironically. One imagines that groups of farmers mingled their voices to this ballad while enjoying some home-brewed beer after a taxing day in those stoney New England fields.

A West-country Mans Voyage, in dialect, was originally printed in a compendium of English ballads and records, as a faithful Anglican's reactions to Congregational ceremonial innovations in New England. When put side by side these songs represent rather nicely some of the attitudes of those who ruefully remained in New England and those who left. We can only wish that many more such popular works had survived.

W.H.K.

[33]

ANONYMOUS,

NEW ENGLAND'S ANNOYANCES

[1640]

New England's annoyances[1] you that would know them,
Pray ponder these verses which briefly do show them.
The place where we live is a wilderness wood,
Where grass is much wanting that's fruitful and good.

From the end of November till three months are gone,
The ground is all frozen as hard as a stone.
Our mountains and hills and our valleys below
Being commonly covered with ice and with snow.

And when the northwest wind with violence blows,
Then every man pulls his cap over his nose:
But if any's so hardy and will it withstand,
He forfeits a finger, a foot, or a hand.

But when the spring opens, we then take the hoe
And make the ground ready to plant and to sow;
Our corn being planted and seed being sown,
The worms destroy much before it has grown.

And while it is growing some spoil there is made
By birds and by squirrels that pluck up the blade.
And when it is come to full corn in the ear,
It is often destroyed by racoon and by deer.

1. Harrison T. Meserole, ed., *Seventeenth Century American Poetry* (Garden City: Anchor Books, 1968), pp. 503–05.

And now our apparel begins to grow thin,
And wool is much wanted to card and to spin.
If we get a garment to cover without,
Our other ingarments are clout upon clout.[2]

Our clothes we brought with us are apt to be torn,
They need to be clouted before they are worn.
But clouting our garments doth injure us nothing:
Clouts double are warmer then single whole clothing.

If fresh meat be wanting to fill up our dish,
We have carrots and pumpkins and turnips and fish;
And if there's a mind for a delicate dish,
We haste to the clam banks and take that we wish.

Stead of pottage and puddings and custards and pies,
Our turnips and parsnips are common supplies.
We have pumpkins at morning and pumpkins at noon,
If it was not for pumpkins, we should be undone.

(If barley be wanting to make into malt,
We must be contented and think it no fault;
For we can make liquor to sweeten our lips
Of pumpkins and parsnips and walnut tree chips.)

And of our green cornstalks we make our best beer,
We put in it barrels to drink all the year.
Yet I am as healthy, I verily think,
Who make the spring water my commonest drink.

Our money's soon counted, for we have just none,
All that we brought with us is wasted and gone.
We buy and sell nothing but upon exchange,
Which makes all our dealings uncertain and strange.

2. Patch upon patch.

[35]

And we have a cov-nant one with another
Which makes a division 'twixt brother and brother:
For some are rejected and others made saints,
Of those that are equal in virtues and wants.

For such like annoyances we've many mad fellows
Find fault with our apples before they are mellow,
And they are for England, they will not stay here,
But meet with a lion in shunning a bear.

Now while such are going, let others be coming,
Whilst liquor is boiling, it must have a scumming.
And I will not blame them, for birds of a feather
Are choosing their fellows by flocking together.

But you whom the Lord intends hither to bring
Forsake not the honey for fear of a sting:
But bring both a quiet and contented mind,
And all needful blessings you surely shall find.

A WEST-COUNTRY MANS VOYAGE TO

NEW-ENGLAND

[1670]

A West-country Mans Voyage to New-England[3]
My Masters give audience, and listen to me,
And streight che will tell you where che have be:
Che have been in New-England, but now cham come o'er,
Itch do think they shal catch me go thither no more.

3. *Merry Drollerie Complete* (London: for Simon Miller, 1670), pp. 275–77.

Before che went o'er Lord how Voke did tell
How vishes did grow, and how birds did dwell
All one mong, t'other in the wood and the water;
Che thought had been true, but che find no such matter.

When first che did land che mazed me quite,
And 'twas of all daies on a Satterday night,
Che wondered to see the strong building were there,
'Twas all like the standing at *Bartholmew* Fair.[4]

Well, that night che slept till near Prayer time,
Next morning che wondered to hear no Bells chime,
And when che had ask'd the reason, che found
'Twas because they had never a Bell in the Town.

At last being warned to Church to repair,
Where che did think certain che sho'd hear some prayer,
But the Parson there no such matter did teach,
They scorn'd to pray, they were all able to preach.

The virst thing they did, a Zalm they did sing,
I pluckt out my Zalm book, which with me did bring,
Che was troubled to seek him, cause they called him by name,
But they had got a new Song to the tune of the same.

When Sermon was done was a child to baptize
About sixteen years old, as volk did surmise,
And no Godfather nor Godmother, yet 'twas quiet and still,
The Priest durst not cross him for fear of his ill will.

4. A fair held on the 24th of August at West Smithfield in commemoration of the Apostle.

[37]

ASirra, quoth I, and to dinner che went,
And gave the Lord thanks for what he had sent;
Next day was a wedding, the brideman my friend
He kindly invites me, so thither I wend.

But this, above all, to me wonder did bring,
To see a Magistrate marry, and had ne'r a ring,
Che thought they would call me the woman to give,
But che think he stole her, for he askt no man leave.

Now this was new *Dorchester* as they told me,
A Town very famous in all that Country;
They said 'twas new building, I grant it was true,
Yet methinks old *Dorchester* as fine as the new.

Che staid there among them till che was weary at heart,
At length there came shipping, che got leave to depart;
But when all was ended che was coming away,
Che had three score shillings for swearing to pay.

But when che saw that, an oath more cheswore,
Che would stay no more longer to swear on the score;
Che bid farewell to those Fowlers and Fishers,
So God bless old *England* and all his well wishers.

THE

SIMPLE COBLER

OF

AGGAWAM IN AMERICA.

NATHANIEL Ward was born in England around 1578, but the exact date remains obscure despite biographical searching.[1] He trained as a lawyer and was admitted to the bar in 1615. After a tour of the continent, Ward abandoned his profession to become a nonconformist Puritan minister at Stondon-Massey in Essex. Driven from this pastorate for his dissenting opinions, he emigrated to Massachusetts in 1634 where be became pastor at Aggawam (Ipswich), Massachusetts. Failing health and difficulties in adjusting to frontier life led Ward to quit his post and move to Boston where he played an important role in the creation of the first "Body of Liberties," the codified laws of the colony. Homesick for an England which was increasingly dominated by Puritanism, Ward left North America in 1646, as did many another transplanted pastor.[2]

Ward seems to have written *The Simple Cobler* in 1636 at Ipswich. It was a public admonishment to Charles I to espouse the True Faith and restore religious sanity to the realm. As such, Ward posed as a humble shoemaker with the effrontery to criticize a king. One mustn't go too far toward an Americanistic or democratic interpretation of Ward's presumption; it emerged from the Puritan revolution in England which Ward abandoned America to rejoin. Still, his satiric sermon was written in America, thereby illustrating how transatlantic developments merged in our humorous traditions.

1. Jean Beranger, *Nathaniel Ward* (ca. 1578–1652), (Bordeaux, France: Société bordelaise de travaux des lettres et sciences humanies, 1969), p. 43.
2. Harry S. Stout, "University Men in New England 1620–1660: A Demographic Analysis," *Journal of Interdisciplinary History,* IV, 3 (Winter 1974), 375–400.

The major comic effects in *The Simple Cobler* are achieved through punning, word play, word invention, and, of course, the satiric mask. Exaggeration is employed for ridicule and Ward likens humans to animals, a persistent theme in colonial humorous writing. *The Simple Cobler* indulges a very intellectual wit, by comparison with later writers, and rarely creates a visual image to produce laughter. Indeed, the laughter was intended to be hard, brutal, ironic, and even sarcastic. The ultimate goal was not the enjoyment of mirth but moral reformation. Since humor and the drive for reformed manners both persisted, Ward's bizarre book went through four editions in England and a fifth in early eighteenth-century Boston. The following excerpt is taken from the last, Boston edition.

W.H.K.

SUTOR ULTRA CREPIDEM.[3]

EITHER I am in Apoplexy, or that man is in a Lethargy, who doth not now sensibly feel God shaking the Heavens over his head, and the Earth under his feet: The Heavens so, as the Sun begins to turn into darkness, the Moon into blood, the Stars to fall down to the ground; . . . the foundations are failing, the righteous scarce know where to find rest, the inhabitants stagger like drunken men. . . .

Satan is now in his passions, he feels his passion approaching: he loves to fish in royled waters. . . .

First, such as have given or taken any unfriendly reports of us *New-English,* should doe well to recollect themselves. We have been reputed a Colluvies[4] of wild Opinionists, swarmed into a remote wilderness to find elbow-room for our Phanatick Doctrines and Practices: I trust our diligence past, and constant sedulity against such persons and courses, will plead better things for us. I

3. A Shoemaker (who works) above the Shoe [Sutor Ultra Crepidam].
4. Collections or gatherings of filth or foul matter.

dare take upon me, to be the Herauld of *New-England* so far, as to proclaim to the World, in the name of our Colony, that all Familists, Antinomians, Anabaptists, and other Enthusiasts shall have free Liberty to keep away from us, and such as will come to be gone as fast as they can, the sooner the better.

Secondly, I dare aver, that God doth no where in his word tolerate Christian States, to give Tolerations to such adversaries of his Truth, if they have power in their hands to suppress them.

Here is lately brought us an Extract of a *Magna Charta,* so called, compiled between the Sub-planters of a *West-Indian* Island; whereof the first Article of constipulation, firmly provides free stable-room and litter for all kind of Consciences, be they never so dirty or jadish, making it actionable, yea, treasonable, to disturb any man in his Religion, or to discommend it, whatever it be. We are very sorry to see such professed Prophaneness in *English* Professors [believers], as industriously to lay their Religious foundations on the ruins of true Religion; . . . God abhorring such loathsome beverages, hath in his righteous judgment blasted that enterprize, which might otherwise have prospered well, for ought I know; I presume their case is generally known ere this. [5]

. . . My heart hath naturally detested four things: The standing of the Apocrypha in the Bible; Forainers dwelling in my Country, to crowd out Native Subjects into the corners of the Earth; Alchymized Coines; Tolerations of divers Religions, or of one Religion in segregant shapes: He that willingly assents to the last, if he examines his heart by day-light, his Conscience will tell him, he is either an Atheist, or an Heretick, or an Hypocrite, or at best a captive to some Lust; Poly-piety is the greatest impiety in the World.

. . . if the State of *England* shall either willingly Tolerate, or weakly connive at such Courses, the Church of that Kingdom will sooner become the Devils dancing-School, than Gods Temple: The Civil State a Bear-garden, than an Exchange: The whole

5. Ward probably refers to Bermuda.

[41]

Realm a Pais base[6] than an *England*. And what pity it is, that that Country which hath been the Staple of Truth to all Christendom, should now become the Aviary of Errors to the whole World, let every fearing heart judge. . . .

There is talk of an universal Toleration, I would talk as loud as I could against it, did I know what more apt and reasonable Sacrifice *England* could offer to God for his late performing all his heavenly Truths than an universal Toleration of all hellish Errors, or how they shall make an universal Reformation, but by making Christs Academy the Devils University, where any man may commence Heretick *per saltum* [by leaping]; where he that is *filius Diabolicus* [son of the Devil], or simpliciter pessimus [even worse], may have his grace to go to Hell *cum Publico Privilegio* [as a public privilege]; and carry as many after him, as he can.

Religio docenda est, non coercenda[7] is a pretty piece of *album Latinum*[8] for some kind of throats that are willingly sore, but *Haeresis dedocenda est non permittenda,*[9] will be found a far better *Diamoron*[10] for the Gargarismes[11] this Age wants, if timely and th[o]roughly applyed.

If there be room in *England* for

Familists		Manes
Libertines		Lemures
Erastians		Dryades
Antitrinitarians		Homadryades
Anabaptists		Potamides
Antiscripturists		Naiades
Arminians		Hinnides
Manifestarians	the room	Pierides
Millinarians	for	Nereides
Antinomians		Pales

---

6. A play on the French for Low Countries; normally *pays bas*.
7. Religion is to be taught, not forced.
8. Latin cliche.
9. Teaching heresy is forbidden.
10. A mixture of mulberry juice and syrup used as a gargle for sore throats.
11. French for mouthwash, but without the 'e'.

Socinians		Anonides
Arrians		Parcades
Perfectists		Castalides
Brownists		Monides
Mortalians		Charites
Seekers	Good Spirits,	Heliconides
Enthusiasts	but very Devils	Pegasides
		&c.

Religious Men but
pernicious Hereticks

In a word room for Hell above ground.[12]

It is said, That Men ought to have Liberty of their Conscience, and that it is Persecution to debar them of it: I can rather stand amazed than reply to this: it is an astonishment to think that the braines of men should be parboyl'd in such impious ignorance; Let all the wits under the Heavens lay their heads together and find an Assertion worse than this (one excepted) I will Petition to be chosen the universal Ideot of the World.

. . . But why dwell I so intolerable long about Tolerations, I hope my fears are but Panick, against which I have a double cordial. . . . let the petty Chapmen [Small Merchants] make their Market while they may, . . . He that sitteth in the Heavens laughs at them, the most High hath them in Derision, and their folly shall certainly be manifested to all men.

. . . every Prophet, to whom God hath given the Tongue of the Learned, should teach, and every Angel who hath a Pen and Inkhorn by his side write against these grieving extravagancies: writing of many Books, I grant is irksome, reading endless. A reasonable man would think Divines had declaimed sufficiently upon these Themes. I have ever thought the Rule given, *Titus* 3.10.[13] which cuts the work short and sharp to be more properly prevalent, than wearisome waiting upon unweariable Spirits.

12. Ward did not complete his thought, but appears to have meant that were there acceptance of such a motley, England, and New England, would be damned.
13. "A man that is an heretike, after the first and second admonition avoid."

[43]

It is a most toylesome task to run the wild-goose chase after a well breath'd Opinionist: they delight in vitilitigation [contention]: it is an itch that loves to be scrub'd: they desire not satisfaction, but satisdiction, whereof themselves must be judges: yet in new eruptions of Error with new objections, silence is sinful. . . .

Here I hold my self bound to set up a Beacon, to give warning of a new-sprung Sect of Phrantasticks, which would perswade themselves and others, that they have discovered the North-west passage to Heaven. These wits of the game, cry up and down in Corners such bold ignotions of a new Gospel, new Christ, new Faith, and new gay nothings . . . he that would be delivered, let him avoid these blasphemers, a late fry of croaking Frogs, not to be indured in a Religious State, no, if it were possible, not an hour.

. . . An easie head may soon demonstrate, that the Prementioned Planters, by Tolerating all Religions, had immazed themselves in the most intolerable confusions and inextricable thraldoms the World ever heard of. I am perswaded the Devil himself was never willing with their proceedings, for fear it would break his wind and wits to attend such a Province. I speak it seriously, according to my meaning. How all Religions should enjoy their liberty Justice its due regularity, Civil cohabitation moral honesty, in one and the same Jurisdiction, is beyond the Attique of my comprehension. If the whole conclave of Hell can so compromise, exadverse, and diametrical contradictions, as to compolitize such a multimonstrous maufrey of heteroclytes and quicquidlibets quietly; I trust I may say with all humble reverence, they can do more than the Senate of Heaven. . . .

Should I not keep Promise in speaking a little to Womens fashions, they would take it unkindly: I was loath to pester better matter with such stuff; I rather thought it meet to let them stand by themselves, like the *Quae Genus* [what Gender] in the Grammar, being Deficients, or Redundants, not to be brought under any Rule: I shall therefore make bold for this once, to borrow a little of their loose tongued Liberty, and mispend a word or two upon their long-wasted, but short-skirted Patience: a little use of my stirrup will do no harm.

[44]

Ridentem dicare verum, quid prohibet?[14]

> *Gray Gravity it self can well be team,*
> *That Language be adapted to the Theme.*
> *He that to Parrots speaks, must parrotize:*
> *He that instructs a fool, may act th' unwise.*

It is known more than enough, that I am neither Nigard, nor Cinick, to the due bravery of the true Gentry: if any man mistakes a bullymong drossock [a sloppily dressed woman] more than I, let him take her for his labour: I honour the Woman that can honour her self with her attire: a good Text always deserves a fair Margent; I am not much offended, if I see a trimme far trimmer than she that wears it: in a word, whatever Christianity or Civility will allow, I can afford with *London* measure: but when I hear a nugiperous [inventing trifles] Gentledame inquire what dress the Queen is in this week: what the nudiustertian [of the day before yesterday] fashion of the Court; with egge to be in it in all haste, what ever it be; I look at her as the very gizzard of a trifle, the product of a quarter of a cypher, the epitome of Nothing, fitter to be kickt, if she were of a kickable substance, than either honour'd or humour'd.

To speak moderately, I truly confess it is beyond the ken of my understanding to conceive, how those Women should have any true Grace, or valuable vertue, that have so little wit, as to disfigure themselves with such exotick garbes, as not only dismantles their native lovely lustre, but transclouts [disfigures with patches] them into gantbar-geese [gaping geese], ill-shapen-shotten [emaciated] shellfish, Egyptian Hyeroglyphicks, or at the best into French flurts of the pastery, which a proper English Woman should scorne with her heels: it is no marvel they wear drailes [long, trailing head-dresses] on the hinder part of their heads, having nothing as it seems in the fore-part, but a few Squirrils brains to help them frisk from one ill-favour'd fashion to another.

14. "What's to keep me from telling the truth with a laugh?"

[45]

These whimm' Crown'd shees, these fashion-fansying wits,
Are empty thin brain'd shells, and fidling Kits.

The very troublers and impoverishers of mankind, I can hardly forbear to commend to the World a saying of a Lady living some-time with the Queen of *Bohemia,* I Know not where she found it, but it is pity it should be lost.

The World is full of care, much like unto a bubble,
Women and Care, and care and Women, and
Women and care and trouble.

The Verses are even enough for such odd pegma's,[15] I can make my self sick at any time, with comparing the dazling splender wherewith our Gentlewomen were imbellished in some former habits, with the gut-foundred goofdom, wherewith they are now surcingled [girded] and debauched. We have about five or six of them in our Colony: if I see any of them accidentally, I cannot cleanse my phansie of them for a Month after. I have been a solitary Widdower almost twelve years, purposed lately to make a step over to my Native Country for a yoke-fellow: but when I consider how Women there have tripe-wised themselves with their cladments, I have no heart to the Voyage, least their nauseous shapes and the Sea, should work too sorely upon my stomach. I speak sadly; methinks it should break the hearts of English men, to see so many goodly English women imprisoned in French Cages, peering out of their hood holes for some men of mercy to help them with a little wit, and no body relieves them.

It is a more common than convenient saying, that nine Taylors make a man: it were well if nineteen could make a Woman to her mind: if Taylors were men indeed, well furnished but with meer Moral Principles, they would disdain to be led about like Apes, by such mymick Marmosets. It is a most unworthy thing, for men that have bones in them, to spend their lives in making fidle-cases for futilous [futile] Womens phansies; which are the very *pettitoes*

15. A moveable theater stage.

[pig's feet] of Infirmity, the giblets of perquisquilian [trifling, worthless] toyes. I am so charitable to think, that most of that mystery would work the cheerfuller while they live, if they might be well discharged of the tyring slavery of mis-tyring Women: it is no little labour to be continually putting up English-women, into Outlandish caskes; who if they be not shifted a new, once in a few Months, grow too sowre for their Husbands. What this Trade will answer for themselves when God shall take measure of Taylors Consciences is beyond my skill to imagine. There was a time when,

> *The joyning of the Red-Rose with the White,*
> *Did set our State into a Damask plight.*

But now our Roses are turned to *Flore de lices,* our Carnations to Tulips, our Gilliflowers to Dayzes, our City Dames, to an indenominable Quaemalry of over-turcas'd [over-turquoised] things. He that makes Coates for the Moon, had need take measure every Noon: and he that makes for Women as often, to keep them from Lunacy.

I have often heard divers Ladies vent loud feminine complaints of the wearisome varieties and chargeable changes of fashions: I marvel themselves prefer not a Bill of redress. I would *Essex* Ladies would lead the *Chore,* for the honour of their Country and Persons; or rather the thrice honourable Ladies of the Court, whom it best beseems: who may well presume of a *Le Roy le veult* from our sober King, a *Les Seigneurs ont assentus* from our prudent Peers, and the like *Assentus,* from our considerate, I dare not say Wife-worn Commons: who I believe had much rather pass one such Bill, than pay so many Taylors Bills as they are forced to doe.

Most dear and unparallel'd Ladies, be pleased to attempt it: as you have the precellency of the Women of the World for beauty and feature; so assume the honour to give, and not take Law from any, in matter of attire: if ye can transact so fair a motion among your selves unanimously, I dare say, they that most renite [resist pressure] will least repent. What greater honour can your Honours desire, than to build a Promontory president to all foraigne Ladies,

[47]

to deserve so eminently at the hands of all the English Gentry present and to come: and to confute the opinion of all the wise men in the world; who never thought it possible for women to doe so good a work?

If any man think I have spoken rather merrily than seriously he is much mistaken, I have written what I wrote with all the indignation I can, and no more than I ought. I confesse I veer'd my tongue to this kinde of Language *de industria* [diligently] though unwillingly, supposing those I speak to are uncapable of grave and rationall arguments. . . .

THE JOURNAL OF

MADAM KNIGHT

SARAH Kemble Knight was born in Boston, Massachusetts, on April 19, 1666, one of five or six children in the family of Thomas and Elizabeth Kemble. The family was "of the middling sort" and known primarily for providing refuge to wandering strangers and indigents.[1] Sarah, who outlived all the other children, married one Richard Knight, an artisan, whom she also survived. Her daughter married well, bringing Widow Knight into the family of John Livingston of New York. After an active life of shop-keeping, land speculation, and inn-keeping, Sarah Kemble Knight died in New London, Connecticut on September 25, 1727.

These none-too-detailed facts illuminate somewhat the following journal which she kept of her trip on horseback to New London and New York City and back, in late 1704 and (by our calendar) early 1705. The author never specified the nature of her goals, referring only to some family and business reasons. The bulk of her acerbic comments was reserved for the inns and taverns at which she "baited" and the regularity or irregularity of the towns through which she passed. As an inn-keeper and land owner herself, Mrs. Knight seems to have combined her business acumen with her comic eye, thus laughing in the knowledge of how much better a job she had, or might have, done in the areas she visited. In any event, her humorous observations were quite naturally made in the course of other affairs and give us one of the most intimate glimpses of early American humor.

When one combines the facts of her daughter's successful mar-

1. Malcolm Freiberg, ed., *The Journal of Madam Knight* (Boston: D. R. Godine, 1972), pp. iii–vii.

riage to the leading landholding family of New York with the mother's caustic comments on the many socially inferior types she met on her voyage to New York, humor helps clarify the process of Puritan "tribalism" which tended to locate salvation along genealogical lines.[2] "Bumkin Simpers" and "Jone Tawdry" were perfect foils for the right sort of people who through the Half-Way Covenant were destined to rule New England despite their failure to receive spiritual election. Widow Knight paid scant attention to the spiritual states of those she met but showed little doubt that she, at least, preferred those who lived decorously in the "clean houses" of established New England communities.

The tone of Sarah Kemble Knight's journal, however, injects an ingredient so painfully absent from the holy laughter of Nathaniel Ward, for Mrs. Knight found herself slightly funny, as well as those whom she encountered. A frail but persevering female dependent upon various strange guides in finding her way through unfamiliar territory, Sarah Knight found strength in laughter. The long, hard trip and her reactions to it were tests of humor's functional role in wilderness survival. This good woman not only survived, but persevered with great style.

W.H.K.

Monday, Octb'r Ye Second, 1704.—About three o'clock afternoon, I began my Journey from Boston to New-Haven; being about two Hundred Mile. My Kinsman, Capt. Robert Luist, waited on me as farr as Dedham, where I was to meet ye Western post.

I vissitted the Reverd. Mr. Belcher, ye Minister of ye town, and tarried there till evening, in hopes ye post would come along. But he not coming, I resolved to go to Billingses where he used to lodg, being 12 miles further. But being ignorant of the way, Madm Billings, seing no persuasions of her good spouses or hers could prevail with me to Lodg there that night, Very kindly went wyth me to ye Tavern, where I hoped to get my guide, And desired the Hostess to inquire of her guests whether any of them would go with mee. But they being tyed by the Lipps to a pewter engine, scarcely

2. See Edmund S. Morgan, *The Puritan Family* (New York: Harper & Row, 1966).

allowed themselves time to say what clownish . . . (*manuscript torn at this point*) . . . Peices of eight, I told her no, I would not be accessary to such extortion.

Then John shan't go, sais shee. No, indeed, shan't hee; And held forth at that rate a long time, that I began to fear I was got among the Quaking tribe,[3] beleeving not a Limbertong'd sister among them could out do Madm. Hostes.

Upon this, to my no small surprise, son John arrose, and gravely demanded what I would give him to go with me? Give you, sais I, are you John? Yes, says he, for want of a Better [name]; And indwdl this John look't as old as my Host, and perhaps had bin a man in this last Century. Well, Mr. John, sais I, make your demands. Why, half a pss. of eight and a dram, sais John. I agreed, and gave him a Dram (now) in hand to bind the bargain,

My hostess catechis'd John for going so cheep, saying his poor wife would break her heart. . . . His shade of his Hors resembled a Globe on a Gate post. His habitt, Hors and furniture, its looks and goings Incomparably answered the rest.

Thus Jogging on with an easy pace, my Guide telling mee it was dangero's to Ride hard in the Night, (whch his horse had the sence to avoid,) Hee entertained me with the Adventurs he had passed by late Rideing, and eminent Dangers he had escaped, so that, Re-membring the Hero's in Parismus and the Knight of the Oracle,[4] I didn't know but I had mett wth a Prince disguis'd.

When we had Ridd an how'r, wee come into a thick swamp, wch. by Reason of a great fogg, very much startled mee, it being now very Dark. But nothing dismay'd John: Hee had encountered a thousand and a thousand such Swamps, having a Universall Knowledge in the woods; and readily Answered all my inquiries wch. were not a few.

In about an how'r, or something more, after we left the Swamp, we come to Billinges, where I was to Lodg. My Guide dismounted

3. Quakers or the Society of Friends.
4. *Works of the Elizabethan writer, Emmanuel Ford: The most Famous, Delectable, and pleasant, History of Parismus, the most renowned Prince of Bohemia* . . . (1598); *The Famous History of Montelion, Knight of the Oracle* (1633). See Perry Miller and Thomas H. Johnson, *The Puritans* (New York: American Book Co., 1938), p. 776.

and very Complasantly help't me down and shewd the door, signing to me wth his hand to Go in; wch I Gladly did—But had not gone many steps into the Room, ere I was Interogated by a young Lady I understood afterwards was the Eldest daughter of the family, with these, or words to this purpose, (viz.) Law for mee—what in the world brings You here at this time a night?—I never see a woman on the Rode so Dreadfull late, in all the days of my versall [whole] life. Who are you? Where are You going? I'me scar'd out of my witts—with much now of the same Kind. I stood aghast, Prepareing to reply, when in comes my Guide—to him Madam turn'd, Roreing out: Lawfull heart, John, is it You?—how de do! Where in the world are you going with this woman? Who is she? John made no Ansr. but sat down in the corner, fumbled out his black Junk [pipe], and saluted that instead of Debb; she then turned agen to mee and fell anew into her silly questions, without asking me to sitt down.

I told her shee treated me very Rudely, and I did not think it my duty to answer her unmannerly Questions. But to get ridd of them, I told her I come there to have the post's company with me tomorrow on my Journey, &c. Miss star'd awhile, drew a chair, bid me sitt, And then run up stairs and putts on two or three Rings, (or else I had not seen them before,) and returning, sett herself just before me, showing the way to Reding, that I might see her Ornaments, perhaps to gain the more respect. But her Granam's new Rung sow,[5] had it appeared would affected me as much. I paid honest John wth money and dram according to contract, and Dismist him, and pray'd Miss to shew me where I must Lodg. Shee conducted me to a parlour in a little back Lento [lean-to], wch was almost fill'd wth the bedsted, wch was so high that I was forced to climb on a chair to gitt up to ye wretched bed that lay on it; on wch having Stretcht my tired Limbs, and lay'd my head on a Sadcolourd pillow, I began to think on the transactions of ye past day.

TUESDAY, OCTOBER Ye THIRD . . . about two, after-

5. A pig with a ring in its snout.

noon, Arrived at the Post's second stage . . . Here, having called for something to eat, ye woman bro't in a Twisted thing like a cable, but something whiter; and laying it on the bord, tugg'd for life to bring it into a capacity to spread; wch having wth great pains accomplished, shee serv'd in a dish of Pork and Cabage, I suppose the remains of Dinner. The sause was of a deep Purple, wch I tho't was boil'd in her dye Kettle; the bread was Indian, and every thing on the Table service Agreeable to these. I, being hungry, gott a little down; but my stomach was soon cloy'd, and what cabbage I swallowed serv'd me for a Cudd the whole day after.

   . . . About Three afternoon went on with my Third Guide, who Rode very hard; and having crossed Providence Ferry, we come to a River wch they Generally Ride thro'. But I dare not venture; so the Post got a Ladd and Cannoo to carry me to tother side, and hee rid thro' and Led my hors. The Cannoo was very small and shallow, so that when we were in she seem'd redy to take in water, which greatly terrified mee, and caused me to be very circumspect, sitting with my hands fast on each side, my eyes stedy, not daring so much as to lodg my tongue a hair's breadth more on one side of my mouth then tother, nor so much as think on Lott's wife, [Genesis 19:26] for a wry thought would have oversett our wherey: But was soon put out of this pain, by feeling the Cannoo on shore, wch I as soon almost saluted with my feet; and Rewarding my sculler, again mounted and made the best of our way forwards. . . . the Post told mee we had neer 14 miles to Ride to the next Stage, (where we were to Lodg.) I askt him of the rest of the Rode, foreseeing wee must travail in the night. Hee told mee there was a bad River we were to Ride thro', wch was so very firce a hors could sometimes hardly stem it: But it was but narrow, and wee should soon be over. I cannot express The concern of mind this relation sett me in: no thoughts but those of the dang'ros River could entertain my Imagination, and they were as formidable as varios, still Tormenting me with blackest Ideas of my Approaching fate—Sometimes seing my self drowning, otherwhiles drowned, and at the best like a holy Sister Just come out of a Spiritual Bath in dripping Garments.

[53]

. . .

I gave Reins to my Nagg; and sitting as Stedy as Just before in the Cannoo, in a few minutes got safe to the other side, which hee told mee was the Narragansett country.'

. . .

From hence wee kept on, with more ease yn before: the way being smooth and even, the night warm and serene. . . .

. . . Being come to mr. Havens', I was very civilly Received, and courteously entertained, in a clean comfortable House; and the Good woman was very active in helping off my Riding clothes, and then ask't what I would eat. I told her I had some Chocolett, if shee would prepare it; which with the help of some Milk, and a little clean brass Kettle, she soon effected to my satisfaction. I then betook me to my Apartment, wch was a little Room parted from the Kitchen by a single bord partition; where, after I had noted the Occurances of the past day, I went to bed, which, tho' pretty hard, Yet neet and handsome. But I could get no sleep, because of the Clamor of some of the Town tope-ers in next Room, Who were entred into a strong debate concerning ye Signifycation of the name of their Country, (viz.) *Narraganset*. One said it was named so by ye Indians, because there grew a Brier there, of a prodigious Highth and bigness, the like hardly ever known, called by the Indians Narrangansett; And quotes an Indian of so Barberous a name for his Author, that I could not write it. His Antagonist Replyed no—It was from a Spring it had its name, wch hee well knew where it was, which was extreem cold in summer, and as Hott as could be imagined in the winter, which was much resorted too by the natives, and by them called Narragansett, (Hott and Cold,) and that was the originall of their places name—with a thousand Impertinances not worth notice, wch He utter'd with such a Roreing voice and Thundering blows with the fist of wickedness on the Table, that it peirced my very head. I heartily fretted, and wish't t'um tongue tyed; but wth as little succes as a friend of mine once, who was (as shee said) kept a whole night awake, on a Jorny, by a country Left. and a Sergent, Insigne and a Deacon, contriving how to bring a

[54]

triangle into a Square. They kept calling for tother Gill, wch while they were swallowing, was some Intermission; But presently, like Oyle to fire, encreased the flame. I set my Candle on a Chest by the bed side, an setting up, fell to my old way of composing my Resentments, in the following manner:

> I ask thy Aid, O Potent-Rum!
> To Charm these wrangling Topers Dum.
> Thou hast their Giddy Brains possest-
> The man confounded wth the Beast-
> And I, poor I, can get no rest.
> Intoxicate them with thy fumes:
> O still their Tongues till morning comes!

And I know not but my wishes took effect; for the dispute soon ended wth' tother Dram; and so Good night!

WEDNESDAY, OCTOBr 4th. About four in the morning, we set out for Kingston (for so was the Town called) with a french Docter in our company. Hee and ye Post put on very furiously, so that I could not keep up with them, only as now and then they'd stop till they see mee. This Rode was poorly furnished wth accommodations for Travellers, so that we were forced to ride 22 miles by the post's account, but neerer thirty by mine, before wee could bait so much as our Horses, wch I exceedingly complained of. But the post encourag'd mee, by saying we should be well accommodated anon at mr. Devills, a few miles further. But I questioned whether we ought to go to the Devil to be helpt out of affliction. However, like the rest of Deluded souls that post to ye Infernal denn, Wee made all posible speed to this Devil's Habitation; where alliting, in full assurance of good accommodation, wee were going in. But meeting his two daughters, as I suposed twins, they so neerly resembled each other, both in features and habit, and look't as old as the Divel himselfe, and quite as Ugly, We desired entertainm't, but could hardly get a word out of 'um, till with our Importunity, telling them our necesity, &c. they call'd the old Sophister, who was as sparing of his words as his daughters had bin, and no, or none, was the

[55]

reply's hee made us to our demands. Hee differed only in this from the old fellow in to'ther Country: hee let us depart. However, I thought it proper to warn poor Travailers to endeavour to Avoid falling into circumstances like ours, wch at our next Stage I sat down and did as followeth:

> May all that dread the cruel feind of night
> Keep on, and not at this curs't Mansion light.
> 'Tis Hell; 'tis Hell! and Devills here do dwell:
> Here dwells the Devill—surely this's Hell.
> Nothing but Wants; a drop to cool yo'r Tongue
> Cant be procur'd these cruel Feinds among.
> Plenty of horrid Grins and looks sevear,
> Hunger and thirst, But pitty's banish'd here—
> The Right hand keep, if Hell on Earth you fear!

Thus leaving this habitation of cruelty, we went forward; and arriving at an Ordinary about two mile further, found tollerable accommodation. But our Hostes, being a pretty full mouth'd old creature, entertain'd our fellow travailer, ye french Docter, wth Inumirable complaints of her bodily infirmities; and whisperd to him so lou'd, that all ye House had as full a hearing as hee: which was very divirting to ye company, (of which there was a great many,) as one might see by their sneering. But poor weary I slipt out to enter my mind in my Journal, and left my Great Landly with her Talkative Guests to themselves.

From hence we proceeded . . . and . . . came to . . . a little cottage Just by the River, to wait the Waters falling, wch the old man that lived there said would be in a little time, and he would conduct me safe over. This little Hutt was one of the wretchedest I ever saw a habitation for human creatures. . . . Notwithstanding both the Hutt and its Inhabitance were very clean and tydee: to the crossing the Old Proverb, that bare walls make giddy[6] howswifes. . . .

---

6. English proverb: "Bare walls make gadding housewives."

[56]

I had scarce done thinking, when an Indian-like Animal come to the door, on a creature very much like himself, in mien and feature, as well as Ragged cloathing; and having 'litt, makes an Awkerd Scratch wth his Indian shoo, and a Nodd, sitts on ye block, fumbles out his black Junk, dipps it in ye Ashes, and presents it piping hott to his muscheeto's, and fell to sucking like a calf, without speaking, for near a quarter of an hower. At length the old man said how do's Sarah do? who I understood was the wretches wife, and Daughter to ye old man: he Replyed—as well as can bc cxpected, &c. So I remembred the old say, and suposed I knew Sarah's case. Butt hee being, as I understood, going over the River, as ugly as hee was, I was glad to ask him to show me ye way to Saxtons, at Stonington; . . . Here I heard there was an old man and his Daughter to come that way, bound to N. London; and being now destitute of a Guide, gladly waited for them, being in so good a harbour, and accordingly, . . . I sat forward with neighbour Polly and Jemima, a Girl about 18 Years old, who hee said he had been to fetch out of the Narragansetts, and said they had Rode thirty miles that day, on a sory lean Jade, wth only a Bagg under her for a pillion, which the poor Girl often complain'd was very uneasy.

Wee made Good speed along, wch made poor Jemima make many a sow'r face, the mare being a very hard trotter; and after many a hearty and bitter Oh, she at length Low'd out: Lawful Heart father! this bare mare hurts mee Dingeely [bruisingly], I'me direfull sore I vow; with many words to that purpose: poor Child sais Gaffer—she us't to serve your mother so. I don't care how mother us't to do, quoth Jemima, in a pasionate tone. At which the old man Laught, and kik't his Jade o' the side, which made her Jolt ten times harder.

About seven that Evening, we come to New London Ferry: here, by reason of a very high wind, we mett with great difficulty in getting over—the Boat tos't exceedingly, and our Horses capper'd at a very surprizing Rate, and set us all in a fright; especially poor Jemima, who desired her father to say [']so jack['] to the Jade, to make her stand. But the careless parent, taking no notice of her repeated desires, She Rored out in a Passionate manner: [']Pray

[57]

suth father, Are you deaf? Say so Jack to the Jade, I tell you.[*] The Dutiful Parent obey's, saying [*]so Jack, so Jack,[*] as gravely as if hee'd bin to saying Catechise after Young Miss, who with her fright look't of all coullers in ye Rain Bow.

.   .   .

FRIDAY, OCTOr 6th. . . . come to an ordinary, [where we] were well entertained by a woman of about seventy and vantage, but of as Sound Intellectuals as one of seventeen. Shee entertain'd Mr. Wheeler wth some passages of a Wedding awhile ago at a place hard by, the Brides-Groom being about her Age or something above, Saying his children was dredfully against their fathers marrying, wch shee condemned them extreemly for.

From hence wee went pretty briskly forward, and arriv'd at Saybrook ferry about two of the Clock afternoon; and crossing it, wee call'd at an Inn to Bait, (foreseeing we should not have such another Opportunity till we come to Killingsworth.) Landlady come in, with her hair about her ears, and hands at full pay scratching. Shee told us shee had some mutton wch shee would broil, wch I was glad to hear; But I supose forgot to wash her scratchers [hands]; in a little time shee brot it in; but it being pickled, and my Guide said it smelt strong of head sause, we left it, and pd sixpence a piece for our Dinners, wch was only smell. . . .

SATURDAY, OCT. 7TH, . . . about two a clock afternoon we arrived at New Haven, where I was received with all Posible Respects and civility. . . .

They are govern'd by the same Laws as wee in Boston, (or little differing,) thr'out this whole Colony of Connecticot, And much the same way of Church Government, and many of them good, Sociable people, and I hope Religious too: but a little too much Independant in their principalls, and, as I have been told, were formerly in their Zeal very Riggid in their Administrations towards such as their Lawes made Offenders, even to a harmless Kiss or Innocent merriment among Young people. Whipping being a frequent and counted an easy Punishment, about wch as other Crimes, the Judges were absolute in their Sentances. They told

[58]

mee a pleasant story about a pair of Justices in those parts, wch I may not omit the relation of.

A negro Slave belonging to a man in ye Town, stole a hogs head [wooden barrel] from his master, and gave or sold it to an Indian, native of the place. The Indian sold it in the neighbourhood, and so the theft was found out. Thereupon the Heathen was Seized, and carried to the Justices House to be Examined. But his worship (it seems) was gone into the feild, with a Brother in office, to gather in his Pompions [pumpkins]. Whither the malefactor is hurried, And Complaint made, and satisfaction in the name of Justice demanded. Their Worships cann't proceed in form without a Bench: whereupon they Order one to be Imediately erected, which, for want of fitter materials, they made with pompions—which being finished, down setts their Worships, and the Malefactor call'd, and by the Senior Justice Interrogated after the following manner. [']You Indian why did You steal from this man? You sho'dn't do so—it's a Grandy wicked thing to steal.['] [']Hol't Hol't,['] cryes Justice Junr Brother, [']You speak negro to him. I'le ask him. You sirrah, why did You steal this man's Hoggshead?['] [']Hoggshead?['] (replys the Indian,) [']me no stomany [understand⟨?⟩ steal⟨?⟩].['] [']No?['] says his Worship; and pulling off his hatt, Patted his own head with his hand, sais, [']Tatapa[']—[']You, Tatapa—you; all one this. Hoggshead all one this.['] [']Hah!['] says Netop, [']now me stomany that.['] Whereupon the Company fell into a great fitt of Laughter, even to Roreing. Silence is comanded, but to no effect: for they continued perfectly Shouting. [']Nay,['] sais his worship, in an angry tone, [']if it be so, *take mee off the Bench.*[']

Their Diversions in this part of the Country are on Lecture days and Training days mostly: on the former there is Riding from town to town.

And on training dayes The Youth divert themselves by Shooting at the Target, as they call it, (but it very much resembles a pillory,) where hee that hitts neerest the white has some yards of Red Ribbin presented him, wch being tied to his hattband, the two ends streeming down his back, he is Led away in Triumph, wth great applause, as the winners of the Olympiack Games. . . .

[59]

. . . they Generally lived very well and comfortably in their famelies. But too Indulgent (especially ye farmers) to their slaves: sufering too great familiarity from them, permitting ym to sit at table and eat with them, (as they say to save time,) and into the dish [goes] the black hoof as freely as the white hand. . . .

Being at a merchants house, in comes a tall country fellow, wth his alfogeos [cheeks] full of Tobacco; for they seldom Loose their Cudd, but keep Chewing and Spitting as long as they'r eyes are open, — he advanc't to the midle of the Room, makes an Awkward Nodd, and spitting a Large deal of Aromatic Tincture, he gave a scrape with his shovel like shoo, leaving a small shovel full of dirt on the floor, made a full stop, Hugging his own pretty Body with his hands under his arms, Stood staring rown'd him, like a Catt let out of a Baskett. At last, like the creature Balaam Rode on,[7] he opened his mouth and said: have You any Ribinen for Hatbands to sell I pray? The Questions and Answers about the pay being past, the Ribon is bro't and opened. Bumpkin Simpers, cryes its confounded Gay [excellent quality] I vow; and beckning to the door, in comes Jone Tawdry, dropping about 50 curtsees, and stands by him: hee shows her the Ribin. *Law, You,* sais shee, *its right Gent,* do You, take it, *tis dreadfull pretty.* Then she enquires, *have You any hood silk I pray?* wch being brought and bought, Have You any *thred silk to sew it wth* says shee, wch being accomodated wth they Departed. They Generaly stand after they come in a great while speachless, and sometimes dont say a word till they are askt what they want, which I Impute to the Awe they stand in of the merchants, who they are constantly almost Indebted too; and must take what they bring without Liberty to choose for themselves; but they serve them as well, making the merchants stay long enough for their pay.

We may Observe here the great necessity and bennifitt both of Education and Conversation; for these people have as Large a portion of mother witt, and sometimes a Larger, than those who have bin brought up in Citties; But for want of emprovements,

7. See *Numbers,* xxii-xxiv.

Render themselves almost Ridiculos, as above. I should be glad if they would leave such follies, and am sure all that Love Clean Houses (at least) would be glad on't too. . . .

. . . wee come to Fairfield . . . the Inhabitants . . . have aboundance of sheep, whose very Dung brings them great gain, with part of which they pay their Parsons sallery, And they Grudg that, prefering their Dung before their minister. They Lett out their sheep at so much as they agree upon for a night; the highest Bidder always caries them, And they will sufficiently Dung a Large quantity of Land before morning. But were once Bitt by a sharper who had them a night and sheared them all before morning— . . . Being got to Milford, it being late in the night, I could go no further; . . . The people here go very plain in their apparel (more plain than I had observed in the towns I had passed) and seem to be very grave and serious. They told me there was a singing Quaker[8] lived there, or at least had a strong inclination to be so, His Spouse not at all affected that way. Some of the singing Crew come there one day to visit him, who being then abroad, they sat down (to the woman's no small vexation) Humming and singing and groneing after their conjuring way—Says the woman are you singing quakers? Yea says They—Then take my squalling Brat of a child here and sing to it says she for I have almost split my throat wth singing to him and cant get the Rogue to sleep. They took this as a great Indignity, and mediately departed. Shaking the dust from their Heels left the good woman and her Child among the number of the wicked.

. . . wee got safe home to Boston, where I found my aged and tender mother and my Dear and only Child in good health with open arms redy to receive me . . . and now I cannot fully express my Joy and Satisfaction. But desire sincearly to adore my Great Benefactor for thus graciously carying forth and returning in safety his unworthy handmaid.

8. The followers of George Fox formed themselves into the Society of Friends but were called "Quakers" derogatorily by outsiders who claimed that they shook and moaned in the fear of the Lord. An offshoot of the Friends witnessed the Inner Light through singing.

ENTERTAINMENT

FOR

A WINTER'S-EVENING

JOSEPH Green (1706–1780) was born in Boston and graduated from Harvard. A merchant by trade, Green enjoyed the reputation of a major wit among his fellows. Moses Tyler recounts the story of the day Green noticed that the Fourth Latin School of Boston was being torn down to make room for a new wing on the adjoining church. Green supposedly composed the following lines on the spot:

> A fig for your learning! I tell you the town,
> To make the church larger, must pull the school down.
> 'Unluckily spoken,' replied Master Birch;
> 'Then learning, I fear, stops the growth of the church.'[1]

As a consequence of such spontaneous, if modest, talents, one of Green's friends wrote his epitaph for him "long before he had need of one."

> Siste, Viator! Here lies one,
> Whose life was whim, whose soul was pun;
> And if you go too near his hearse,
> He'll joke you, both in prose and verse.

Green, whatever his contemporary reputation, was a lesser, if persistent, colonial wit. The interest of the following piece lies in its convivial revelations of the growth of the Masonic Fraternity in the colonies. Originally the brotherhood of stone masons in

---

1. Moses Coit Tyler, *A History of American Literature 1607–1765* (New York: Collier Books, 1962), pp. 306–07.

medieval England and Scotland, the Masons were transformed by the reformation into a social order. The first quarter of the eighteenth century witnessed a period of unprecedented growth for the fraternity and it was at this time that it migrated across the Atlantic. The first American lodge met in Tun Tavern in Philadelphia, where Franklin became a member. Boston in 1733 received the first lodge chartered by the British organization and by the time of the revolution there were at least one hundred lodges in America.

That such a group began to thrive in New England is testimony to the decline of strict Congregational orthodoxy, for the Masons were quite ecumenical in membership. Indeed, Green's lighthearted parody of their migration from tavern to church and back again stresses that this organization was able to unite in brotherhood those who had come to differ bitterly in religious matters. The search for consensus had always characterized New England life and the Masons became a further expression of that regional drive.

Still, the satiric and determinedly secular of mind must have remained uncomfortable in the Puritan commonwealth, for Green, at the time of the revolution, returned to England as a loyalist. Nonetheless, in his little spoof Joseph Green provided a humorous glimpse of the process by which New England moved from piety to secularism.

W.H.K.

ENTERTAINMENT
FOR A WINTER'S - EVENING

O Muse renown'd for story telling,
Fair Clio, leave thy airy dwelling.
Now while the streams like marble stand,
Held fast by winter's icy hand;
Now while the hills are cloth'd in snow;
Now while the keen north-west-winds blow;
From the bleak fields and chilling air

Unto the warmer hearth repair:
Where friends in chearful circle met
In social conversation sit.
Come, *Goddess,* and our ears regale
With a diverting christmas tale.
O come, and in thy verse declare
Who were the men, and what they were,
And what their names, and what their fame,
And what the cause for which they came
To house of God from house of ale,
And how the parson told his tale:
How they return'd, in manner odd,
To house of ale from house of God.
Free Masons, as the story goes,
Have two saints for their patrons chose:
And both Saint Johns, one the *Baptist,*
The other the *Evangelist.*
The Baptist had a *Lodge* which stood
Whilom by Jordan's ancient flood.
But for what secret cause the other
Has been adopted for a *brother,*
They cannot, and I will not say,
Nec scire fas est omnia.[2]

The Masons by procession
Having already honour'd one,
(Thou, to perpetuate their glory,
Clio, didst then relate the story.)
To show the world they mean fair play,
And that each saint should have his day,
Now order store of belly-timber
'Gainst twenty-seventh of *December.*

2. The Lord does not permit us to know everything.

[64]

For that's the day of *Saint John's* feast
Fix'd by the holy *Roman* priest.
They then in mood religious chose
Their *brother of the roll and rose*
The ceremony to commence:
He from the sacred eminence
Must first explain and then apply
The duties of *Free Masonry.*

At length, in scarlet apron drest,
Forth rush'd the morning of the feast;
And now the bells in steeple play,
Hark, ding, dong, bell they chime away;
Until, with solemn toll and steady,
The great bell tells—the parson's ready.

Masons at church! strange auditory!
And yet we have as strange in story.
For saints, as history attests,
Have preach'd to fishes, birds and beasts;
Yea stones so hard, tho' strange, 'tis true,
Have sometimes been their hearers too.
So good *Saint Francis,* man of grace,
Himself preach'd to the *braying race;*
And further, as the story passes,
Address'd them thus—*my brother asses.*

. . .

The crowds attending gaze around,
And awful silence reigns profound.
till from the seat which he'd sat his arse on
Uprose and thus began the parson.

[65]

Right Worshipful, at whose command
Obedient I in *Rostra* stand;
It proper is and fit to show
Unto the crowds that gape below,
Who wonder much, and well they may,
What on th' occasion I can say,
Why in the church are met together,
Especially in such cold weather,
Such folk as never did appear
So overfond of coming there.
Know then, my friends, without more pother,
That these are *Masons,* I'm a Brother.
Masons said I?—yes *Masons Free;*
Their *deeds* and *title* both agree.
While other sects fall out and fight
About a trifling mode or rite,
We firm by *Love* cemented stand,
'Tis *Love* unites us heart and hand.
Love to a party not confin'd,
A *Love* embracing all mankind,
Both catholick and protestant,
The Scots and eke *New-England* saint:
Antonio's[3] followers, and those
Who've *Crispin*[4] for their patron chose,
And them, who to their idol goose
Oft sacrifice the blood of louse.[5]
Those who with razor bright and keen,
And careful hand, each morn are seen
Devoting to *Saint Nicolas*[6]
The manly honours of the face.

. . .

3. The patron of sailors.
4. The patron of shoemakers.
5. Tailors?
6. The patron of barbers.

Rhode-Island's differing, motly tribes,
Far more than Alec Ross describes,
And light that's *new,* and light that's *old*[7]
We in friendly arms enfold,
Free, generous and unconfin'd
To outward shape or inward mind.
The high and low and great and small,
J——s P———ns short and A———n tall,
J——n———n as bulky as a house,
And W———d smaller than a louse,
The grave and merry, dull and witty,
The fair and brown, deform'd and pretty,
We all agree, both wet and dry,
From drunken L——— to sober I.
And *Hugh* ——— But hark, methinks I hear
One shrewdly whisp'ring in my ear;
'Pray, parson, don't affirm but prove;
'Do they all meet and part in love?
'Quarrels oft times don't they delight in,
'And now and then a little fighting?
'Did there not (for the Secret's out)
In the last Lodge arise a rout?
'M——— with a fist of brass
'Laid T———'s nose level with his face,
'And scarcely had he let his hand go
When he receiv'd from T——— a d———d blow.
'Now, parson, when a nose is broken,
'Pray, is it a friendly *sign* or *token?*

'Tis true—but trifling is th' objection,
All general rules have an exception.

7. A reference to the "New Lights" who championed the Great Awakening of 1740 and the "Old Lights" who opposed it.

Oft from themselves the best men vary,
Humanum enim est errare.[8]
But what I've said I'll say again,
And what I say I will maintain:
'Tis *Love,* pure *Love* cements the whole,
Love — of the *Bottle* and the *Bowl.*

But 'tis high time to let you go
Where you had rather be, I know:
And by proceeding I delay
The weightier business of the day;
For eating *solid sense* affords,
Whilst nonsense lurks in many words.
Doubting does oft arise from thinking,
But truth is only found in drinking.
This having said, the reverend vicar
Dismiss'd them to their food and liquor.

From church to *Stone's* they go to eat,
In order walking through the street,
. . .

See B———k before the apron'd throng
Marches with sword and book along;
The stately ram with courage bold,
So stalks before the fleecy fold,
And so the gander, on the brink
Of river, leads his geese to drink,
And so the geese descend, from gab'ling
On the dry land, in stream to dab'ling.

Three with their white sticks next are seen,
One on each side and one between;

8. Because to err is human.

[68]

Plump L———w———s marches on the right,
Round as a hoop, as bottle tight,
With face full orb'd and rosy too;
So ruddy Cynthia oft we view,[9]
When she, from tippling eastern streams,
First throws about her evening beams,

. . .

Who's he comes next?—'Tis P———e by name,
P———e by his nose well known to fame;
This, when the generous juice recruits,
Around a brighter radiance shoots.
So, on some promontory's height,
For Neptune's sons the signal light
Shines fair, and fed by unctuous stream,
Sends off to sea a livelier beam.

But see the crowds, with what amaze
They on the 'pothecary gaze!
'Tis he, when belly suffers twitch,
Caus'd by the too retentive breech,
Adjusts with finger nice and thumb
The ivory tube to patient's bum,

. . .

When'er, for aiding nature frail,
Poor bawd must follow the cart's tail,
As through fair *London's* streets she goes,
The mob, like fame, by moving grows,
They should'ring close, press, stink and shove,
Scarcely can the procession move.
Just such a street-collected throng

9. The Cynthian goddess, i.e., Artemis or Diana, said to have been born on Mount Cynthus; hence the Moon.

[69]

Guarded the *brotherhood* along;
Just such the noise, just such the roar
Heard from behind and from before.
'Till lodg'd at *Stone's,* nor more pursu'd,
The mob with three huzzas conclude.

    And now, withdrawn from publick view,
What did the *brethren* say and do?
Had I the force of *Stentor's* lungs,
A voice of brass, a hundred tongues;
My tongues and voice and lungs would fail,
E'er I had finished half my tale;
E'er I had told their names and nation,
Their virtues, arts and occupation,
Or in fit strains had half made known
What words were spoke, what deeds were done.
Clio, 'tis thou alone, canst show 'em,
For thou'rt a Goddess and must know 'em.

       . . .

PART THREE

Southern Satirical Wit

A

CHARACTER

OF THE PROVINCE OF

MARY - LAND,

GEORGE Alsop was the madcap among early American humorists. We do not know when he was born, although as the first of two sons born to Peter and Rose Alsop of London, this tailor's son was baptized in 1636 at St. Martin's-in-the-Fields.[1] After two years spent as a "Handicraft" apprentice, George Alsop signed an indenture for four years of servitude in Maryland. When he had completed his contract, Alsop returned to England and left few traces thereafter.

Even this short visit, under exacting circumstances, and prompt return do not seem to indicate that the New World had disappointed him. To the contrary, Alsop praised Maryland, where he arrived in December or January, 1658/9, and extolled the virtues of indentured servitude in America. Indeed, part of his quixotic impact lies in his smiling return to England, which he roundly satirized, from Maryland, which he seems to have thoroughly enjoyed.

After his arriving in the proprietary government of the Calvert family, Alsop was indentured to Thomas Stockett who lived near the head of the Chesapeake Bay, south of the Susquehanna River. From this vantage, the author observed all manner of American phenomena, including the local Indians. Surely Alsop was favored above many indentured servants, for it appears from his book that Stockett was a kindly and reasonable master.

Alsop's political and religious views may help to explain his noisy entry and hasty departure from the new world. An unyielding supporter of the Stuart monarchs, he lavished scorn and vitupera-

1. J. A. Leo Lemay, *Men of Letters in Colonial Maryland* (Knoxville: Univ. of Tennessee Press, 1972), p. 48.

tion upon the "roundhead" Puritans, whose short but revolutionary rule in England sent many a "Cavalier" scampering for exile. With the Restoration of 1660, Alsop's beloved monarchy and Anglicanism had returned to power, and he, like other royalists, might go home in triumph. In the meantime, Maryland, which had been granted to the Catholic Calvert family by Charles I, had provided a congenial refuge.

George Alsop used "current literary fashions to win his audience: the background of the new science; the tradition of learned wit, especially the elaborately rhetorical low style characteristic of Thomas Nash; the Restoration frankness about sex; comic word play, including paradox, incongruous personification, extravagantly extended figures of speech, and word coinages, . . ."[2] Moreover, his is an explosive, indeed, chaotic humor. Although he often mocks the accepted *bêtes-noires* of the Royalists, as in his caricature of constipation among the Puritans, he diverges from the expected. Alsop is the first writer in British America to elaborate the engaging stereotype of the uncouth but shrewd American who used his image of ignorance and stupidity to "scalp" snobbish and unsuspecting British merchants. Indeed, for all his praise of Royalist leadership, Alsop's picture of Maryland is refreshingly democratic. In keeping with his unpredictability, this merrymaker goes a long way toward shattering the seventeenth-century hierarchy, which he loved, with the egalitarian axe.

In his *Character of Maryland* Alsop used America as a satiric device in ridiculing England. From the hardened and hardy colonists, living among seven-foot-tall Indian giants in harmonious, industrious plenty, we look back to a cowardly, overcrowded, and foppish England, too torn by war and ignorance to realize the possibilities of her own colonies. In this regard, however short Alsop's sojourn in America, he laid the foundation for future generations of native humorists.

Still, Alsop was too much the blithe spirit to have confined himself to any given politics of humor. His wildly unorganized book, prefaced by innumerable rambling introductions, and bound

2. Lemay, *Men of Letters,* p. 48.

[74]

at the opposite extreme with "Historical Letters" written before he left England, employs humor for its own sake. As its author commented, if the reader found it "wild and confused" it was because he was similarly inclined himself. Happily, Alsop revelled in that particular condition. Basking in his own good spirits, this "Character" of the Province of Maryland left us his "bastard brat" of a book. One doubts that he took it very seriously and there is no reason why its readers should take it in any other light. We may be excused for wondering, however, if Alsop lent it to his parishioners when he became an Anglican minister back in England.

W.H.K.

I am now entring for some time to dwell under the Government of *Neptune,* a Monarchy that I was never manured to live under, nor to converse with in his dreadful Aspect, neither do I know how I shall bear with his rough demands;. . .

I am now bound for *Mary-Land,* and I am told that's a New World, but if it prove no better than this, I shall not get much by my change; but before I'll revoke my Resolution, I am resolv'd to put it to adventure, for I think it can hardly be worse than this is: . . .

I am got ashoar with much ado, and it is very well it is as it is, for if I had stayed a little longer, I had certainly been a Creature of the Water, for I had hardly flesh enough to carry me to Land, not that I wanted for any thing that the Ship could afford me in reason: But oh the great bowls of Pease-porridge that appeared in sight every day about the hour twelve, ingulfed the senses of my Appetite so, with the restringent quality of the Salt Beef upon the internal Inhabitants of my belly, that a *Galenist*[3] for some dayes after my arrival, with his Bagpipes of Physical operations, could hardly make my Puddings dance in any methodical order. . . .

We had a blowing and dangerous passage of it, and for some days after I arrived, I was an absolute *Copernicus,* it being one main

3. A follower of the medical practices of Galen, a second-century physician of Asia Minor.

[75]

point of my moral Creed, to believe the World had a pair of long legs, and walked with the burthen of the Creation upon her back. For to tell you the very truth of it, for some dayes upon Land, after so long and tossing a passage, I was so giddy that I could hardly tread an even step; so that all things both above and below (that was in view) appeared to me like the *Kentish Britains* to *William the Conqueror,*[4] in a moving posture. . . .

Herds of Deer are as numerous in this Province of *Mary-Land,* as Cuckholds can be in *London,* only their horns are not so well drest and tipt with silver as theirs are. . . .

Sir, If you send any Adventure to this Province, let me beg to give you this advice in it; That the Factor whom you imploy be a man of a Brain, otherwise the Planter will go near to make a Skimming-dish of his Skull: I know your Genius can interpret my meaning. The people of this place (whether the saltness of the Ocean gave them any alteration when they went over first, or their continual dwelling under the remote Clyme where they now in-habit, I know not) are a more acute people in general, in matters of Trade and Commerce, then in any other place of the World; and by their crafty and sure bargaining, do often over-reach the raw and unexperienced Merchant. To be short, he that undertakes Mer-chants imployment for *Mary-Land,* must have more of Knave in him than Fool; he must not be a whindling piece [whiner, complainer] of Formality, that will lose his Imployers Goods for Conscience sake; nor a flashy piece of Prodigality, that will give his Merchants fine Hollands, Laces and Silks, to purchase the benevo-lence of a Female: But he must be a man of a solid confidence, carrying alwayes in his looks the Effigies of an Execution upon Command, if he supposes a baffle, or denyal of payment, where a debt for his Imployer is legally due. . . .

The Antimonial Cup[5] (dear Cosen) you sent me, I had; and as soon as I received it, I went to work with the Infirmities and

4. The region of Kent, England was a center of resistance to the conquest and reign of the Norman king, William the Conqueror.
5. Made of glass of antimony, a bluish, white, flakey crystalline, used to heighten the emetic qualities of wine.

[76]

Diseases of my body. At the first draught, it made such havock among the several humors that had stoln into my body, that like a Conjurer in a room among a company of little Devils, they no sooner hear him begin to speak high words, but away they pack, and happy is he that can get out first, some up the Chimney, and the rest down stairs, till they are all disperst. So those malignant humours of my body, feeling the operative power, and medicinal vertue of this Cup, were so amazed at their sudden surprizal, (being alwayes before battered only by the weak assaults of some few Emporicks) they stood not long to dispute, but with joynt consent made their retreat, some running through the sink of the Skullery, the rest climbing up my ribs, took my mouth for a Garret-window, and so leapt out.

To the Right Honorable *Caecilius Lord Baltemore,* Absolute Lord and Proprietary of the Provinces of *Mary-Land* and *Avalon*[6] in *America*

My Lord,

I have adventured on your Lordships acceptance by guess; if presumption has led me into an Error that deserves correction, I heartily beg Indempnity, and resolve to repent soundly for it, and do so no more. What I present I know to be true, *Experientia docet;* It being an infallible Maxim, *That there is no Globe like the occular and experimental view of a Countrey.* And had not Fate by a necessary imployment, confined me within the narrow walks of a four years Servitude, and by degrees led me through the most intricate and dubious paths of this Countrey, by a command-ing and undeniable Enjoynment, I could not, nor should I ever have undertaken to have written a line of this nature.

If I have wrote or composed any thing that's wilde and confused, it is because I am so my self, and the world, as far as I can perceive, is not much out of the same trim; therefore I resolve, if I am brought to the Bar of *Common Law* for any thing I have done here, to plead *Non compos mentis,* to save my Bacon.

6. Southeastern Newfoundland, named after the Arthurian town of Glastonbury (Isle of Avalon) by Lord Baltimore who before founding Maryland, placed an aborted colony there.

There is an old Saying in English, *He must rise betimes that would please every one*. And I am afraid I have lain so long a bed, that I think I shall please no body; if it must be so, I cannot help it. But as *Felton* in his *Resolves* says, *In things that must be, 'tis good to be resolute*; And therefore what Destiny has ordained, I am resolved to wink, and stand to it. So leaving your Honour to more serious meditations, I subscribe my self,

My Lord,
Your Lordship['s] most
Humble Servant,
George Alsop.

To all the Merchant Adventures for MARY-LAND, together with those Commanders of Ships that saile into that Province.
Sirs,
You are both Adventurers, the one of Estate, the other of Life:[7] I could tell you I am an Adventurer too, if I durst presume to come into your Company. I have ventured to come abroad in Print, and if I should be laughed at for my good meaning, it would so break the credit of my Understanding, that I should never dare to shew my face upon the Exchange of (conceited) Wits again.

This dish of Discourse was intended for you at first, but it was manners to let my Lord have the first cut, the Pye being his own. I beseech you accept of the matter as 'tis drest, only to stay your stomachs, and I'le promise you the next shall be better done. 'Tis all as I can serve you in at present, and it may be questionable whether I have served you in this or no. Here I present you with *A Character of Mary-Land,* it may be you will say 'tis weakly done, . . . If I am blamed for what I have done too much, it is the first, and I will irrevocably promise it shall be the last. There's a Maxun upon Tryals at Assizes,[8] That if a Thief be taken upon the first fault, if it be not too hainous, they only burn him in the hand and let him go: So I desire you to do by me, if you find any thing that bears a criminal absurdity in it, only burn me for my first fact and let me

7. The usual terminology was: *Adventurer,* or one who invested in colonizing ventures but remained in England; and *Planter,* one who might invest but who actually migrated.
8. A judicial inquest.

[78]

go. But I am affraid I have kept you too long in the Entry, I shall desire you therefore to come in and sit down.

THE
PREFACE
TO THE
READER.

The Reason why I appear in this place is, lest the general Reader should conclude I have nothing to say for my self; and truly he's in the right on't, for I have but little to say (for my self) at this time: For I have had so large a Journey, and so heavy a Burden to bring *Mary-Land* into *England,* that I am almost out of breath: I'le promise you after I am come to my self, you shall hear no more of me. Good Reader, because you see me make a brief Apologetical excuse for my self, don't judge me; for I am so self-conceited of my own merits, that I almost think I want none. *De Lege non judicandum ex sola linea,* saith the Civilian; We must not pass judgement upon a Law by one line: And because we see but a small Bush⁹ at a Tavern door, conclude there is no Canary. For as in our vulgar Resolves 'tis said, *A good face needs no Band,*¹⁰ and an ill one deserves none: So the French Proverb says, *Bon Vien il n'a faut point de Ensigne,*¹¹ Good Wine needs no Bush. I suppose by this time some of my speculative observers have judged me vainglorious; but if they did but rightly consider me, they would not be so censorious. For I dwell so far from Neighbors, that if I do not praise my self, no body else will: And since I am left alone, I am resolved to summon the *Magna Charta* of Fowles to the Bar for my excuse, and by their irrevocable Statutes plead my discharge, *For its an ill Bird will befoule her own Nest:* Besides, I have a thousand *Billings-gate* Collegians¹² that will give in their tes-

9. English taverns of the period were frequently identified by a "bush" or fir-branch before the door.
10. Shackles or fetters.
11. More precisely: *Bon Vin il ne faut point d'Ensigne* (Good Wine needs no Label).
12. Those who frequented and "studied" the Billings-gate fish market.

timony, *That they never knew a Fish-woman cry stinking Fish.*
Thus leaving the Nostrils of the Citizens Wives to demonstrate
what they please as to that, and thee (Good Reader) to say what
thou wilt, I bid thee Farewel.

The
AUTHOR
To His
BOOK

WHen first Apollo got my brain with Childe,
He made large promise never to beguile,
But like an honest Father, he would keep
Whatever Issue from my Brain did creep:
With that I gave consent, and up he threw
Me on a Bench, and strangely he did do;
Then every week he daily came to see
How his new Physick still did work with me.
And when he did perceive he'd don[e] the feat,
Like an unworthy man he made retreat,
Left me in desolation, and where none
Compassioned when they heard me groan.
What could he judge the Parish then would think,
To see me fair, his Brat as black as Ink?
If they had eyes, they'd swear I were no Nun,
But got with Child by some black *Africk* Son,
And so condemn me for my Fornication,
To beat them Hemp to stifle half the Nation.
Well, since 'tis so, I'le alter this base Fate,
And lay his Bastard at some Noble's Gate;
Withdraw my self from Beadles,[13] and from such,
Who would give twelve pence I were in their clutch:

13. A beadle was a minor parish official.

[80]

Then, who can tell? this Child which I do hide,
May be in time a Small-beer Col'nel *Pride,*
But while I talk, my business it is dumb,
I must lay double-clothes unto thy Bum,
Then lap thee warm, and to the World commit
The Bastard Off-spring of a New-born wit.
Farewel, poor Brat, thou in a monstrous World,
In swadling bands, thus up and down art hurl'd;
There to receive what Destiny doth contrive,
Either to perish, or be sav'd alive.
Good Fate protect thee from a Criticks power,
For if he comes, thou'rt gon[e] in half an hour,
Stifl'd and blasted, 'tis their usual way,
To make that Night, which is as bright as Day.
For if they once but wring, and skrew their mouth,
Cock up their Hats, and set the point Du-South,
Armes all a kimbo, and with belly strut,
As if they had *Parnassus* in their gut:
These are the Symptomes of the murthering fall
Of my poor Infant, and his burial.
Say he should miss thee, and some ign'rant Asse
Should find thee out, as he along doth pass,
It were all one, he'd look into thy Tayle,
To see if thou wert Feminine or Male;
When he'd half starv'd thee, for to satisfie
His peeping Ign'rance, he'd then let thee lie;
And vow by's wit he ne're could understand,
The Heathen dresses of another Land;
Well, 'tis no matter, wherever such as he
Knows one grain, more than his simplicity.
Now, how the pulses of my Senses beat,
To think the rigid Fortune thou wilt meet;
Asses and captious Fools, not six in ten

[81]

Of thy Spectators will be real men,
To Umpire up the badness of the Cause,
And screen my weakness for the rav'nous Laws,
Of those that will undoubted sit to see
How they might blast this new-born Infancy;
If they should burn him, they'd conclude hereafter,
'Twere too good death for him to dye a Martyr;
And if they let him live, they think it will
Be but a means for to encourage ill,
And bring in time some strange *Antipod'ans*[14]
A thousand Leagues beyond *Philippians,*
To storm our Wits; therefore he must not rest,
But shall be hang'd, for all he has been prest:
Thus they conclude.—My Genius comforts give,
In Resurrection he will surely live.

. . .

MARY-LAND is a Province situated upon the large extending bowels of *America,* under the Government of the Lord *Baltemore* . . . being within her own imbraces extraordinary pleasant and fertile. Pleasant, in respect of the multitude of Navigable Rivers and Creeks that conveniently and most profitably lodge within the armes of her green, spreading, and delightful Woods; whose natural womb (by her plenty) maintains and preserves the several diversities of Animals that rangingly inhabit her Woods; as she doth otherwise generously fructifie this piece of Earth with almost all sorts of Vegetables, as well Flowers with their varieties of colours and smells, as Herbes and Roots with their several effects and operative vertues, that offer their benefits daily to supply the want of the Inhabitant, whene're their necessities shall Sub-poena them to wait on their commands. . . . So that had Nature made it her business, on purpose to have found out a situation for the Soul of profitable Ingenuity, she could not have fitted herself better in the

14. Those who dwell directly opposite to each other on the globe, so that the soles of their feet are as it were planted against each other; i.e. direct opposites.

traverse of the whole Universe, not in convenienter terms have told man, *Dwell here, live plentifully and be rich.*

The Trees, Plants, Fruits, Flowers, and Roots that grow here in *Mary-Land,* are the only Emblems or Hieroglyphicks of our Adamitical or Primitive situation, . . . which by their dumb vegetable Oratory, each hour speaks to the Inhabitant in silent acts, That they need not look for any other Terrestrial Paradice . . . I shall forbear to particularize those several sorts of Vegetables that flourishingly grows here, by reason of the vast tediousness that will attend upon the description, which therefore makes them much more fit for an Herbal,[15] then a small Manuscript or History.

As for the wilde Animals of this Country . . . *videlicet,* the Deer . . . The Gentleman whom I served my conditional and prefixed time withall, had at one time in his house fourscore Venisons, besides plenty of other provisions to serve his Family nine months, they being but seven in number; so that before this Venison was brought to a period by eating, it so nauseated our appetites and stomachs, that plain bread was rather courted and desired than it.

The Deer here neither in shape nor action differ from our Deer in *England:* The Park they traverse their ranging and unmeasured walks in, is bounded and impanell'd in with no other pales then the rough and billowed Ocean: They are also mighty numerous in the Woods, and are little or not at all affrighted at the face of a man, but (like the Does of *Whetstons* Park)[16] though their hydes are not altogether so gaudy to extract an admiration from the beholder, yet they will stand (almost) till they be scratcht.

As for the Wolves, Bears, and Panthers of this Country . . . they are hardly worth mentioning: For the highest of their designs and circumventing reaches is but cowardly and base, only to steal a poor Pigg, or kill a lost and half starved Calf. The Effigies of a man terrifies them dreadfully, for they no sooner espy him but their hearts are at their mouths, and the spurs upon their heels, they

15. A treatise on plants.
16. A gathering place for prostitutes in London, this area was actually a narrow roadway in the parish of St. Giles-in-the-fields.

[83]

(having no more manners then Beasts) gallop away, and never bid them farewell that are behind them.

. . . this Land or Government of *Mary-Land* may boast, that she enjoys as much quietness from the disturbance of Rebellious Opinions, as most States or Kingdoms do in the world: For here every man lives quietly, . . . and by the protection of the Laws, they are supported from those molestious troubles that ever attend upon the Commons of other States and Kingdoms, as well as from the Aquasortial [draining] operation of great and eating Taxes. . . . the thin jawed Skeliton with his starv'd Carkess is never seen walking the Woods of *Mary-Land* to affrighten Children. . . .

Here Suits and Tryals in Law seldom hold dispute two Terms of Courts, but according as the Equity of the Cause appears is brought to a period. The *Temples* and *Grays-Inne* [law schools] are clear out of fashion here: *Marriot*[17] would sooner get a paunch-devouring meal for nothing, then for his invading Counsil. Here if the Lawyer had nothing else to maintain him but his bawling, he might button up his Chops, and burn his Buckrom Bag [a lawyer's bag], or else hang it upon a pin untill its Antiquity had eaten it up with durt and dust: Then with a Spade, like his Grandsire *Adam,* turn up the face of the Creation, Purchasing his bread by the sweat of his brows, that before was got by the motionated Water-works of his jaws. . . .

. . . Here the Constable hath no need of a train of Holberteers [armed guards], that carry more Armour about them, then heart to guard him: Nor is he ever troubled to leave his Feathered Nest to some friendly successor, while he is placing of his Lanthern-horn Guard at the end of some suspicious Street, to catch some Night-walker, or Batchelor of Leachery, that has taken his Degree three story high in a Bawdy-house. Here's no *Newgates*[18] for pilfering Felons, nor *Ludgates*[19] for Debtors, nor any *Bride-wels*[20] to lash

17. Probably a lawyer.
18. A prison for thieves in London.
19. A prison for debtors in London.
20. A forced-labor prison in London.

the soul of Concupiscence into a chast Repentance. For as there is none of these Prisons in *Mary-Land,* so the merits of the Country deserves none, but if any be foully vitious, he is so reserv'd in it, that he seldom or never becomes popular. . . . These Christian Natives of the Land, especially those of the Masculine Sex, are generally conveniently confident, reservedly subtle, quick in apprehending, but slow in resolving; and where they spy profit sailing towards them with the wings of a prosperous gale, there they become much familiar. The Women differ something in this point, though not much: They are extreme bashful at the first view, but after a continuance of time hath brought them acquainted, there they become discreetly familiar, and are much more talkative then men. All Complemental Courtships, drest up in critical Rarities, are meer strangers to them, plain wit comes nearest their Genius; so that he that intends to Court a *Mary-Land* Girle, must have something more then the Tautologies of a long-winded speech to carry on his design, or else he may (for ought I know) fall under the contempt of her frown, and his own windy Oration.

. . . Now those whose abilities here in *England* are capable of maintaining themselves in any reasonable and handsom manner, they had best so to remain, lest the roughness of the Ocean, together with the staring visages of the wilde Animals, which they may see after their arrival into the Country, may alter the natural dispositions of their bodies, that the stay'd and solid part that kept its motion by Doctor *Trigs* purgationary operation, may run beyond the byas of the wheel in a violent and laxative confusion.

. . .

The Women that go over into this Province as Servants, have the best luck here as in any place of the world besides; for they are no sooner on shoar, but they are courted into a Copulative Matrimony, which some of them (for ought I know) had they not come to such a Market with their Virginity, might have kept it by them untill it had been mouldy, unless they had let it out by a yearly rent to some of the Inhabitants of Lewknors-lane,[21] or made a Deed of

21. A Rendezvous and nursery for prostitutes, now Charles St., Drury Lane.

Gift of it to Mother *Coney*, [22] having only a poor stipend out of it, untill the Gallows or Hospital called them away. Men have not altogether so good luck as Women in this kind, or natural preferment, without they be good Rhetoricians, and well vers'd in the Art of Perswasion, then (probably) they may ryvet themselves in the time of their Servitude into the private and reserved favour of their Mistress, if Age speak their Master deficient. . . .

. . . I have observed on the other side of *Mary-Land,* that the whole course of most Mechanical endeavors, is to catch, snatch, and undervalue one another, to get a little work, or a Customer; . . .

Then did not a cloud of low and base Cowardize eclipse the Spirits of these men, these things might easily be diverted; but they had as live take a Bear by the tooth, as think of leaving their own Country, though they live among their own National people, and are governed by the same Laws they have here, yet all this wont do with them; and all the Reason they can render to the contrary is, There's a great Sea betwixt them and *Mary-Land,* and in that Sea there are Fishes, and not only Fishes but great Fishes, and then should a Ship meet with such an inconsiderable encounter as a Whale, one blow with his tayle, and then *Lord have Mercy upon us:* Yet meet with these men in their common Exchange, which is one story high in the bottom of a Cellar, disputing over a Black-pot [beer mug] it would be montrously dreadful here to insert the particulars, one swearing that he was the first that scaled the Walls of *Dundee,* [23] when the Bullets flew about their ears as thick as Hail-stones usually fall from the Sky; which if it were but rightly examined, the most dangerous Engagement that ever he was in, was but at one of the flashy battels at *Finsbury,* [24] where commonly there's more Custard greedily devoured, then men prejudiced by the rigour of the War. Others of this Company relating their several dreadful exploits, and when they are just entring into the particu-

22. Literally, a Rabbit, but figuratively a coarse reference to a Madame.
23. The town was repeatedly sacked as late as 1651. No renowned walls are associated with it.
24. A borough of London. Also a training area for local musters.

[86]

lars, let but one step in and interrupt their discourse, by telling them of a Sea Voyage, and the violency of storms that attends it, and that there are no back-doors to run out at, which they call, *a handsom Retreat and Charge again;* the apprehensive danger of this is so powerful and penetrating on them, that a damp sweat immediately involves their Microcosm, so that *Margery* the old Matron of the Cellar, is fain to run for a half-peny-worth of *Angelica* [an aromatic plant] to rub their nostrils; and though the Port-hole of their bodies has been stopt from a convenient Evacuation some several months, they'le need no other Suppository to open the Orifice of their Esculent faculties then this Relation, as their Drawers or Breeches can more at large demonstrate to the inquisitive search of the curious.

Now I know that some will be apt to judge, that I have written this last part out of derision to some of my poor Mechanick Country-men: Truly I must needs tell those to their face that think so of me, that they prejudice me extremely, by censuring me as guilty of any such crime: What I have written is only to display the sordidness of their dispositions, who rather then they will remove to another Country to live plentiously well, and give their Neighbors more Elbow-room and space to breath in, they will croud and throng upon one another, with the pressure of a beggarly and unnecessary weight. . . .

Trafique, Commerce, and Trade, are those great wheeles that by their circular and continued motion, turn into most Kingdoms of the Earth the plenty of abundant Riches that they are commonly fed withall: . . .

Paracelsus [25] might knock down his Forge, if Trafique and Commerce should once cease, and grynde the hilt of his Sword into Powder, and take some of the Infusion to make him so valorous, that he might cut his own Throat in the honor of *Mercury: Galen* might then burn his Herbal, and like Joseph of Arimathea,[26] build him a Tomb in his Garden, and so rest from his labours: Our

25. A Swiss physician, 1490–1541.
26. A Jewish disciple of Christ in whose sepulchre the body of Jesus was laid. Arimathea is five miles north of Jerusalem.

[87]

Physical Collegians of *London* would have no cause then to thunder Fire-balls at *Nich. Culpeppers* Dispensatory: All Herbs, Roots, and Medicines would bear their original christening, that the ignorant might understand them: *Album grecum* would not be *Album grecum* then, but a Dogs turd would be a Dogs turd in plain terms, in spight of their teeth.

If Trade should once cease, the Custom-house would soon miss her hundreds and thousands Hogs-heads[27] of Tobacco, that use to be throng in her every year, as well as the Grocers would in their Ware-houses and Boxes, the Gentry and Commonalty in their Pipes, the Physician in his Drugs and Medicinal Compositions: The (leering) Waiters for want of imployment, might (like so many *Diogenes)*[28] intomb themselves in their empty Casks, and rouling themselves off the Key into the *Thames,* there wander up and down from tide to tide in contemplation of *Aristotles* unresolved curiosity, until the rottenness of their circular habitation give them a *Quietus est,*[29] and fairly surrender them up into the custody of those who both for profession, disposition and nature, lay as near claim to them, as if they both tumbled in one belly, and for name they jump alike, being according to the original translation both *Sharkes.*

. . .

Our Shops and Exchanges of *Mary-Land,* are the Merchants Store-houses, where with few words and protestations Goods are bought and delivered; not like those Shop-keepers Boys in *London,* that continually cry, *What do ye lack Sir? What d' ye buy?* yelping with so wide a mouth, as if some Apothecary had hired their mouths to stand open to catch Gnats and Vagabond Flyes in.

Tobacco is the current Coyn of *Mary-Land,* and will sooner purchase Commodities from the Merchant, then money. I must confess the *New-England* men that trade into this Province, had rather have fat Pork for their Goods, then Tobacco or Furrs; which

27. A wooden cask or barrel for transporting tobacco.
28. The Greek cynic philosopher who supposedly showed his contempt for amenities by living in a tub.
29. A sense of calm, or, figuratively, death.

[88]

I conceive is, because their bodies being fast bound up with the cords of restringent Zeal, they are fain to make use of the lineaments of this *Non-Canaanite* creature physically to loosen them; for a bit of a pound upon a two-peny Rye loaf, according to the original Receipt, will bring the costiv'st red-ear'd Zealot in some three hours time to a fine stool, if methodically observed.

. . .

Barbadoes, together with the several adjacent Islands, has much Provision yearly from this Province: And though these Sun-burnt *Phaetons* think to outvye *Mary-Land* in their Silks and Puffs, daily speaking against her whom their necessities makes them beholding to, and like so many *Don Diegos* that becackt *Pauls,* [30] cock their Felts and look big upon't; yet if a man could go down into their infernals, and see how it fares with them there, I believe he would hardly find any other Spirit to buoy them up, then the ill-visaged Ghost of want, that continually wanders from gut to gut to feed upon the undigested rynes of Potatoes. . . .

As the diversities of Languages (since *Babels* confusion) has made the distinction between people and people, in this Christendom-part of the world; so are they distinguished Nation from Nation, by the diversities and confusion of their Speech and Languages here in *America:* And as every Nation differs in their Laws, Manners and Customs, in *Europe, Asia* and *Africa,* so do they the very same here; That it would be a most intricate and laborious trouble, to run (with a description) through the several Nations of *Indians* here in *America,* considering the innumerableness and diversities of them that dwell on this vast and unmeasured Continent: But rather then I'le be altogether silent, I shall do like the Painter in the Comedy, who being to limne out the Pourtraiture of the Furies, as they severally appeared, set himself behind a Pillar, and between fright and amazement, drew them by guess. Those *Indians* that I have convers'd withall here in this Province of *Mary-Land,* and have had any occular experimental

30. As a noun, "Don Diego" meant Spaniard; as a verb, to cheat. St. Paul is thought, by some, to have evangelized Spain before his martyrdom. Mainland colonists often thought of the Islanders as particularly wanton.

[89]

view of either of their Customs, Manners, Religions, and Absurdities, are called by the name of *Susquehanocks,* [31] being a people lookt upon by the Christian Inhabitants, as the most Noble and Heroick Nation of *Indians* that dwell upon the confines of *America;* also are so allowed and lookt upon by the rest of the *Indians,* by a submissive and tributary acknowledgement; being a people cast into the mould of a most large and Warlike deportment, the men being for the most part seven foot high in latitude, and in magnitude and bulk suitable to so high a pitch; their voyce large and hollow, as ascending out of a Cave; their gate and behavior strait, stately and majestick, treading on the Earth with as much pride, contempt, and disdain to so sordid a Center, as can be imagined from a creature derived from the same mould and Earth.

. . . he that is most cruelly Valorous, is accounted the most Noble: Here is very seldom any creeping from a Country Farm, into a Courtly Gallantry, by a sum of money; nor seeing the Heralds to put Daggers and Pistols into their Armes, to make the ignorant believe that they are lineally descended from the house of the Wars and Conquests; he that fights best carries it here.

. . .

Before I bring my Heathenish Story to a period, I have one thing worthy your observation: For as our Grammer Rules have it, *Non decet quenquam* [*quemquam*] *me ire currentem aut mandantem:* It doth not become any man to piss running or eating. These Pagan men naturally observe the same Rule; for they are so far from running, that like a Hare, they squat to the ground as low as they can, while the Women stand bolt upright with their armes a Kimbo, performing the same action, in so confident and obscene a posture, as if they had taken their Degrees of Entrance at *Venice,* and commenced Bawds of Art at *Legorne.* [32]

31. A tribe of Indians usually associated with the river valley in Pennsylvania.
32. Lieorno, Italy.

THE SOTWEED FACTOR, &c.

EBENEZER Cook, author of *The Sotweed Factor*[1] and a few other, less successful works of satire, shares George Alsop's historical obscurity. Both men are remembered for the humorous writings they left behind them, but the most diligent searching reveals little of the authors themselves.[2] Cook, the son of Andrew Cook 2d and Anne Bowyer, was the third generation of his family to live in Maryland. Each generation, however, plowed back and forth across the ocean, for Ebenezer's father and grandfather seem to have been merchants and brokers in London as well as middling land owners in provincial Maryland. Scholars estimate that Ebenezer was born sometime between 1665 and 1670 on the family plantation "Malden," in Dorchester County, east of the Chesapeake Bay. Raised and educated in England, the satirist may or may not have been a lawyer and it is no more certain that he actively participated in the tobacco economy of the colony. Out of such mystery, John Barth found ample latitude for a fictional elaboration of Ebenezer Cook's unrecorded wanderings through the world.[3]

The *Sotweed Factor* (London, 1708; Annapolis, Md., 1731) takes its literary form from Samuel Butler's (1612–1680) *Hudibras,*[4] but its content is thoroughly colonial. Indeed, in keeping with the author's own wanderlust, the poem concerns the arrival,

1. Lawrence C. Wroth, *The Maryland Muse by Ebenezer Cooke: A Facsimile with an Introduction* (Worcester: American Antiquarian Society, 1935).
2. I am indebted to the fine research and kindness of Edward Cohen of Rollins College for sending me galley proofs of his forthcoming book on Ebenezer Cook.
3. *The Sot-Weed Factor* (New York: Grosset & Dunlap, 1966).
4. J. A. Leo Lemay, *Men of Letters in Colonial Maryland* (Knoxville, Tenn.: Univ. of Tennessee Press, 1972), p. 85n.

subsequent misadventures, and ultimately bitter departure from Maryland of an English merchant ("factor") in the tobacco ("sotweed") trade. Like George Alsop, Cook turned his satire against both the old world and the new, but the emphasis here is clearly on America. Cook contrasts the effete, pompous, and ultimately naive Englishman with the coarse, corrupted, and always slyly deceitful Southern colonists. As a satiric allegory, the destruction of the old world by the new is very complete, yet there are no ultimate triumphs, no moral lessons, and certainly no rhapsodic hymns to the new-found paradise of the American wilderness.

In this regard, *The Sotweed Factor* fully shares the ambiguity of pre-revolutionary American humor: the satirist is buffeted and beleaguered by the raw pretensions of the provinces, but his own "civilized" and European presence remains firmly, even defiantly, unassimilated. Cook, like Knight, Alsop, Byrd, and Hunter, uses humor to survive in the wilderness of ignorance, sloth, greed, and deceit. The laughter, however, is in great measure therapeutic, for America poses few small problems. At the poem's conclusion, Cook's antihero remains stubbornly defiant but Maryland's democratic dogs have nipped close to the bone. It is only through the poem itself, indeed, that Cook can express a satisfying scorn equal to that enjoyed by the American colonists.

I cannot resist the conclusion that *The Sotweed Factor* marks the zenith of pre-revolutionary American humor, and, perhaps, of our humorous writing before Mark Twain. Nowhere else is the wild and bawdy world of the non-New England colonists so vividly captured. Where other writers drew upon similar themes, Cook wove them into an outstandingly colorful fabric, despite his borrowed Butlerian structure.

W.H.K.

CONDEMN'D by Fate, to wayward Curse,
Of Friends unkind, and empty Purse,
Plagues worse than fill'd *Pandora's* Box,
I took my Leave of *Albion's* Rocks,

[92]

With heavy Heart, concern'd that I
Was forc'd my native Soil to fly,
And the old World must bid Good-b'ye:
But Heaven ordain'd it shou'd be so,
And to repine is vain, we know.

FREIGHTED with Fools, from *Plimouth* Sound,
To MARYLAND our Ship was bound;
Where we arriv'd, in dreadful Pain,
Shock'd by the Terrors of the Main;
For full Three Months our wav'ring Boat
Did thro' the surly Ocean float,
And furious Storms and threatening Blasts,
Both split our Sails, and sprung our Masts:
Weary'd, yet pleas'd we did escape
Such Ills, we anchor'd at the *Cape;*
But weighing soon, we plow'd the *Bay,*
To cove it in *Piscataway.* [5]

INTENDING there to open Store,
I put myself and Goods on Shore,
Where soon repair'd a numerous Crew,
In Shirts and Draw'rs, of *Scotch*-cloth blew,
With neither Stocking, Hat, nor Shoe:
These *Sotweed* Planters crowd the Shore,
In Hew as tawny as a *Moor;*
Figures, so strange, no G O D design'd
To be a Part of Human-kind:
But wanton Nature, void of Rest,
Moulded the brittle Clay in Jest.

5. A small river town just south of present-day Washington, D.C.

[93]

AT last, a Fancy very odd,
Took me, This was *The Land of* Nod,
Planted at first when Vagrant *Cain*
His Brother had unjustly slain;
Then, conscious of the Crime he'd done,
From Vengeance dire hither run,
And in a Hut supinely dwelt,
The first in *Furrs* and *Sotweed* dealt:
And ever since that Time, this Place
Has harbour'd a detested Race,
Who, when they could not thrive at Home;
For Refuge to these Worlds did roam,
In Hopes by Flight they might prevent
The Devil, and his fell Intent,
Obtain from Tripple-Tree[6] Reprieve,
And Heav'n and Hell alike deceive:
But e're their Manners I display,
I think it fit I open lay
My Entertainment by the Way,
That Strangers well may be aware on
What homely Diet they must fare on;
To see that Shore where no good sense is found,
But Conversation's lost, and Manners drown'd.

I cross'd unto the other Side
A River, whose impetuous Tide,
Those *Salvage* Borders to divide,
In such a swimming odd Invension,
I scarce can give it's due Dimension,
The *Indians* call this watry Waggon,
Canoe, a Vessel none can brag on,
Cut from a Poplar Tree, or Pine,
And fashion'd like a Trough for Swine:

6. The gallows.

[94]

In this most noble Fishing-boat,
I boldly put my self afloat,
Standing erect, with Legs stretch'd wide,
We paddled to the other Side;
Where being landed safe by Hap,
(As *Sol* fell into *Thetis'* Lap)[7]
A ravenous Gang, bent on the Strowl,[8]
Of Wolves for Prey, began to howl:
This put me in a pannick Fright,
Lest I shou'd be devour'd quite:
But as I there a Musing stood,
And quite benighted in the Wood,
A Female Voice pierc'd thro' my Ears,
Crying, You Rogue drive home the Steers:
I listen'd that attractive Sound,
And streight a Herd of Cattle found,
Drove by a Youth, and homeward bound.
Cheer'd with the Sight, I streight thought fit
To ask, Where I a Bed might get?
The surly Peasant bid me stay,
And ask'd, From whom I'd run away?
Surpris'd at such a sawcy Word,
I instantly lugg'd out my Sword,
Swearing I was no Fugitive,
But from *Great Britain* did arrive,
In hopes I here might better thrive.
To which he mildly made Reply,
I beg your Pardon, Sir, that I
Shou'd talk to you unmannerly:
But if you please to go with me,
To yonder House you'll welcome be.

ENCOUNTERING soon the smoaky Seat,
The Planter old did thus me greet,

7. *Thetis.* The mother of Achilles; poetically, the sea personified.
8. Stroll.

[95]

Whether You're come from Goal, or College,
You're Welcome, to my certain Knowledge,
And if You'll please all Night to stay,
My Son shall put You in the Way:
Which Offer I most kindly took,
And for a Seat did round me look,
When presently among the rest
He plac'd his unknown *English* Guest,
Who found 'em drinking, for a Whet,
A Cask of Sider on the Fret:[9]
'Till Supper came upon the Table,
On which I fed whilst I was able;
So after hearty Entertainment,
Of Drink and Victuals, without Payment,
For Planters Tables, you must know
Are free for all that come and go,
Whilst Pone, with Milk and Mush well stor'd
In wooden Dishes grac'd the Board,
With Hominy and Sider-Pap,
Which scarce an *English* Dog would lap,
Well stuff'd with Fat from Bacon fry'd,
And with Melasses dulcify'd.
Then out our Landlord pulls his Pouch,
As greasy as the Leather Couch
On which he sat, and streight begun
To load with Weed his *Indian* Gun,
In Length scarce longer than one's Finger,
Or that for which the Ladies linger.
His Pipe smoak'd out, with awful Grace,
With Aspect grave and solemn Pace,
The Reverend Sir, walks to a Chest,
Of all his Furniture the best,
Closely confin'd within a Room,
Which seldom felt the Weight of Broom:

9. Cider still in the process of fermentation.

From thence he lugs a Cagg of Rum,
And nodding to me, thus begun:
I find, says he, *you don't much care*
For this our Indian *Country Fare;*
But let me tell you, Friend of mine,
You may be glad of it in Time,
Tho' now you're Stomach is so fine;
And if within this Land you stay,
You'll find it true what I do say:
This said, the Rundlet[10] up he threw,
And bending backwards strongly drew;
I pluck'd as stoutly, for my Part,
Altho' it made me sick at Heart,
And got so soon into my Head,
I scarce could find my Way to Bed;
Where I was instantly convey'd,
By one that pass'd for Chamber-Maid,
Tho' by her loose and sluttish Dress,
She rather seem'd a *Bedlam-Bess.*[11]
Curious to know from whence she came,
I press'd her to declare her Name?
She blushing, seem'd to hide her Eyes,
And thus in civil Terms replies:
In better Times, o'er to this Land
I was unhappily trepann'd,
Perchance as well I did appear,
As any Gentlewoman here,
Not then a Slave for Twice Two Year;
My Cloaths were fashionably new,
Nor were my Shifts of Scotch *Cloth blew:*
But Things are chang'd: Now at the Hoe
I daily work, and barefoot go,

10. Smoke-ring.
11. A female inhabitant of the Hospital of St. Mary of Bethlehem in London—a hospital for lunatics.

[97]

In weeding Corn, and feeding Swine,
I spend my melancholly Time;
Kiknapp'd and fool'd, I hither fled,
To shun a hated Nuptial Bed;
And, to my Grief, already find
Worse Plagues that those I left behind.

WHATE'ER the Wand'rer did profess,
Good faith I cou'd not chuse but guess
The Cause which brought her to this Place,
Was Supping e're the Priest said Grace:
Quick as my Thoughts the Slave was fled,
Her Candle left to shew my Bed,
Which, made of Feathers soft and good,
Close in the Chimney-corner stood:
I laid me down, expecting Rest,
To be in Golden Slumbers blest;
But soon a Noise disturb'd my Quiet,
And plagu'd me with Nocturnal Riot:
A Puss, which in the Ashes lay,
With grunting Pig, began a Fray,
And prudent Dog, that Feuds might cease,
Most sharply bark'd, to keep the Peace:
This Quarrel scarcely was decided
By Stick, that ready lay provided,
But *Reynard,*[12] arch and cunning Loon,
Crept into my Apartment soon,
In hot Pursuit of Ducks and Geese,
With full Intent the same to seize;
Their crackling Plaints with strange Surprise
Chac'd Sleep's thick Vapours from my Eyes;
Raging, I jump'd upon the Floor,
And like a drunken Sailor swore,

12. Fox.

[98]

With Sword I fiercely laid about,
And soon dispers'd the feather'd Rout,
The Poultry out the Window flew,
And *Reynard* cautiously withdrew;
The Dogs who this Encounter heard,
Fiercely themselves to aid me rear'd,
And to the Place of Combat run,
Exactly as the Field was won,
Fretting and hot as roasted Capon,
And greasy as a Flitch of Bacon.

   I to the Orchard did repair,
To breathe the cool and open Air,
Impatient waiting for bright Day,
Extended on a Bank I lay;
But Fortune here, that sawcy Whore,
Disturb'd me worse, and plagu'd me more
Than she had done the Night before;
Hoarse croaking Frogs did round me ring,
Such Peals the Dead to Life wou'd bring,
A Noise might move their Wooden King:
I stuff'd my Ears with Cotton white,
And curs'd the melancholly Night,
For fear of being deaf outright:
But soon my Vows I did recant,
And *Hearing* as a Blessing grant,
When a confounded *Rattle-Snake*
With Hissing made my Heart to ach,
Not knowing how to fly the Foe,
Or whither in the dark to go,
By strange good Luck I took a Tree,
Prepar'd by Fate to set me free,
Where, riding on a Limb astride,
Night and the Branches did me hide,

[99]

And I the De'el and Snake defy'd.
Not yet from Plagues exempted quite,
The curs'd *Muschetoes* did me bite;
'Til rising Morn, and blushing Day,
Drove both my Fears and Ills away,
And from Night's Terrors set me free,
Discharg'd from hospitable Tree.

    I did to Planter's Booth repair,
And there at Breakfast nobly fare,
On Rasher broil'd, of infant Bear:
I thought the Cubb delicious Meat,
Which ne'er did ought but Chesnuts eat,
Nor was young *Orson's*[13] Flesh the worse,
Because he suck'd a *Pagan* Nurse:
Our Breakfast done, the Planter stout,
Handed a Glass of Rum about.

    PLEAS'D with the Treatment I did find,
I took my Leave of Host so kind,
Who, to oblige me, did provide
His eldest Son to be my Guide;
And lent me Horses of his own,
A skittish Colt and aged Roan,
The four legg'd Prop of his Wife *Joan*.
Steering our Course in Trott or Pace,
We sail'd directly for a Place,
In MARYLAND of high Renown;
Known by the name of *Battle-Town:*[14]
To view the crowds did there resort,
Which Justice made, and Law, their Sport,
In their Sagacious County Court:

13. *Ourson,* French for bear cub.
14. This was a town first settled in 1650 on the lower side of the Patuxent River near Battle Creek. Many of the leading families of Maryland settled here. Battle Town, also called Calvertown, was destroyed by the British in 1814.

[100]

Scarce had we enter'd on the Way,
Which thro' the Woods and Marshes lay,
But *Indian* strange did soon appear
In hot Pursuit of wounded Deer;
No mortal Creature can express
His wild fantastick Air and Dress;
His painted Skin, in Colours dy'd,
His sable Hair, in Satchel ty'd,
Show'd *Salvages* not free from Pride:
His tawny Thighs and Bosom bare,
Disdain'd an useless Coat to wear,
Scorn'd Summers Heat and Winters Air;
His manly Shoulders, such as please
Widows and Wives, were bath'd with Grease,
Of Cub and Bear, whose supple Oil,
Prepar'd his Limbs in Heat and Toil.

THUS naked *Pict* in Battle fought,
Or undisguis'd his Mistress sought;
And knowing well his Ware was good,
Refus'd to skreen it with a Hood:
His Visage Dun, and Chin that near
Did Razor feel, nor Scissars bear,
Or know the Ornament of Hair,
Look'd sternly grim; surpriz'd with Fear,
I spurr'd my Horse as he drew near;
But Roan, who better knew than I,
The little Cause I had to fly,
Seem'd by his Solemn Step and Pace,
Resolv'd I shou'd the Spector face,
Nor faster mov'd, tho' spurr'd and prick'd,
Than *Balam's* Ass by Prophet kick'd;

[101]

Keticnatop,[15] the *Heathen* cry'd,
How is it *Tom,* my Friend reply'd;
Judging from thence, the Brute was civil,
I boldly fac'd the courteous Devil,
And lugging out a Dram of Rum,
I gave his tawny Worship some;
Who in his Language as I guess,
My Guide informing me no less,
Implor'd the Devil me to bless:
I thank'd him for his good Intent,
And forward on my Journey went;
Discoursing as along I rode,
Whether this Race was fram'd of GOD,
Or whether some malignant Power,
Had fram'd them in an evil Hour,
And from his own infernal Look,
Their dusky Form and Image took.

   FROM hence we fell to Argument
Whence peopl'd was this Continent?
My Friend suppos'd *Tartarians* wild,
Or *Chinese,* from their home exil'd,
Wandring thro' Mountains hid with Snow,
And Rills that in the Valleys flow,
Far to the *South* of *Mexico,*
Broke thro' the Bars which Nature cast,
And wide unbeaten Regions past;
'Till near those Streams the human Deluge roll'd,
Which sparkling shin'd with glittering Sands of Gold;
And fetch'd *Pisarro* from th' *Iberian* Shore
To rob the *Indians* of their native Store.
   I smil'd to hear my young Logician,
Thus reason like a Politician;

15. "Hello!"

Who ne'r by Father's Pains and Earning,
Had got, at Mother, *Cambridge* Learning;
Where lubber Youth just free from Birch,
Most stoutly drink to prop the Church;
Nor with grey Coat had taken Pains
To purge his Head, and cleanse his Reins;[16]
And in Obedience to the College,
Had pleas'd himself with carnal Knowledge;
And tho' I liked the Younster's Wit,
I judg'd the Truth he had not hit;
And could not chuse but smile to think,
What they cou'd do for Meat and Drink,
Who o'er so many Desarts ran,
With Brats and Wives in Carravan;
Unless perchance they'd got a Trick,
To eat no more than Porker sick,
Or could with well-contented Maws,
Quarter like Bears upon their Paws:
Thinking his Reason to confute,
I gravely thus commenc'd Dispute;
And urg'd, that tho' a *Chinese* host
Might penetrate this *Indian* Coast,
Yet this was certainly most true,
They never could the Isles subdue;
For knowing not to steer a Boat,
They could not on the Ocean float,
Or plant their Sun-burnt Colonies,
In Regions parted by the Seas:
I thence inferr'd, *Phoenicians* old
Discover'd first, with Vessels bold,
These *Western* shores, and planted here,
Returning once or twice a Year,

16. Kidneys.

[103]

With Naval Stores, and Lasses kind,
To comfort those were left behind;
'Till by the Winds and Tempests tore,
From their intended golden Shore,
They suffer'd Shipwreck, or were drown'd,
And lost the World so newly found:
But after long and learn'd Contention,
We could not finish our Dissention;
And when that both had talk'd their Fill,
We had the self same Notion still.

THUS Parson Grave well read, and Sage,
Does in Dispute with Priest engage,
The one protests they are not wise,
Who judge by Sense, and trust their Eyes,
And vows he'd burn for it at Stake,
That man may GOD his Maker make;
The other smiles at his Religion,
And vows he's but a learned Widgeon, [17]
And when they've emptied all their Store,
From Books and Fathers, are not more
Convinc'd, or wiser than before.

SCARCE had we finish'd serious Story,
But I espy'd the Town before me;
And roaring Planters on the Ground,
Drinking of Healths, in Circle round:
Dismounting Steed with friendly Guide,
Our Horses to a Tree we ty'd,
And forward pass'd amongst the Rout,
To chuse convenient Quarters out;
But being none were to be found,
We sat like others on the Ground,

17. Fool.

[104]

Carousing Punch in open Air,
'Till Cryer did the Court declare:
The planting Rabble being met,
Their drunken Worships likewise sat,
Cryer proclaims the Noise shou'd cease,
And streight the Lawyers broke the Peace,
Wrangling for Plaintiff and Defendant,
I thought they ne'r wou'd make an End on't,
With Nonsense, Stuff, and false Quotations,
With brazen Lies, and Allegations;
And in the Splitting of the Cause,
Us'd such strange Motions with their Paws,
As shew'd their Zeal was rather bent
In Blows to end the Argument.
A Reverend Judge, who to the Shame,
Of all the Bench, cou'd write his Name,
At Petty-Fogger took Offence,
And wonder'd at his Impudence:
My Neighbour *Dash,* with Scorn replies,
And in the Face of Justice flies;
The Bench in Fury streight divide,
And Scribles take on Judge's Side;
The Jury, Lawyers, and their Clients,
Contending, fight, like Earth-born Giants,
'Till Sh'riff that slily lay perdue,
Hoping Indictments would ensue;
And when—
A Hat or Wig fell in the Way,
He seiz'd 'em for the Queen, as Stray;
The Court adjourn'd in usual Manner,
In Battle, Blood, and fractious Clamour.

  I though it proper to provide,
A Lodging for my self and Guide,

[105]

So to our Inn we march'd away,
Which at a little Distance lay;
Where all Things were in such Confusion,
I thought the World at it's Conclusion;
A Heard of Planters on the Ground,
O'rewhelm'd with Punch, dead Drunk we found;
Others were fighting and contending,
Some burn'd their Cloaths, to save the mending;
A few whose Heads, by frequent Use,
Could better bear the potent Juice,
Gravely debated State Affairs,
Whilst I most nimbly tripp'd up Stairs,
Leaving my Friend discoursing oddly,
And mixing Things Prophane and Godly;
Just then beginning to be drunk,
As from the Company I slunk:
To every Room and Nook I crept,
In hopes I might have somewhere slept;
But all the Beding was possest,
By one or other drunken Guest;
But after looking long about,
I found an ancient Corn-loft out;
Glad that I might in Quiet sleep,
And there my Bones unfractur'd keep:
I laid me down secur'd from Fray,
And soundly snor'd 'till break o' Day;
When waking fresh, I sat upright,
And found my Shoes were vanish'd quite,
Hat, Wig, and Stockings, all were fled,
From this extended *Indian* Bed:
Vex'd at the Loss of Goods and Chattle,
I swore I'd give the Rascal Battle,
Who had abus'd me in this Sort,

[106]

And Merchant-Stranger made his Sport:
I furiously descended Ladder,
No Hare in *March* was ever madder,
And did with Host and Servants quarrel,
But all in vain, for my Apparel;
For one whose Mind did much aspire
To Mischief, threw them in the Fire.
Equipp'd with neither Hat nor Shoe,
I did my coming hither rue,
And doubtful thoughts what I shou'd do:
When looking round I saw my Friend,
Lye naked on a Table's End,
A Sight so dismal to behold,
One would have thought him dead and cold,
There ready laid, to be next Day
On Shoulders Four convey'd away:
'Till wringing of his bloody Nose,
By fighting got, we may suppose,
I found him not so fast asleep,
Might give his Friends some cause to weep:
Rise *Oronolo,* rise, said I,
And from this *Hell* and *Bedlam* fly:
My Guide starts up, and in a Maze,
With Bloodshot Eyes did round him gaze,
At Lenth with many Sigh and Groan,
He went in search of aged Roan;
But Roan who seldom us'd to falter,
Had fairly this Time slipt his Halter,
And not content all Night to stay,
Ty'd up from Fodder, run away;
After my Guide to catch him ran,
And so I lost both Horse and Man;
Which Disappointment tho' so great,

[107]

Did only Jest and Mirth create:
'Till one more civil than the rest,
In Conversation far the best,
Observing that for want of Roan,
I shou'd be left to walk alone,
Most readily did me intreat,
To take a Bottle at his Seat,
A Favour at that Time so great,
I blest my kind propitious Fate;
And finding soon a fresh Supply
Of Cloaths, from Store-House kept hard by,
I mounted streight on such a Steed,
Did rather Curb than Whipping need;
And straining at the usual Rate,
With Spur of Punch which lies in Pate,
E'er long we lighted at the Gate;
Where in an ancient Cedar-House,
Dwelt my new Friend, a *Cockerouse,*[18]
Whose Fabrick, tho' 'twas built of Wood,
Had many Springs and Winters stood:
When sturdy Oaks and lofty Pines,
Were levell'd with Musk-Melon-Vines,
And Plants eradicated were,
By Hurricans drove in the Air:
There with good Punch and Apple Juice,
We spent out Time without Abuse,
'Till Midnight in her sable Vest,
Persuaded Gods and Men to rest;
And with a pleasing kind Surprize,
Indulg'd soft Slumber to my Eyes.

18. A person of importance in colonial America.

FIERCE *AEthon,*[19] Courser of the Sun,
Had half his Race exactly Run,
And breath'd on me a furious Ray,
Darting hot Beams the following Day,
When Rug in Blanket white, I lay;
But Heat and Chinces[20] rais'd the Sinner,
Most opportunely to his Dinner;
Wild Fowl and Fish delicious Meats,
As good as Neptune's Doxy eats,
Began our hospitable Chear,
Fat Venison follow'd in the Rear,
And Turkeys-wild, luxurious Fare:
But what the Feast did most commend,
Was hearty Welcome from my Friend.

THUS having made a noble Feast,
I eat as well as pamper'd Priest;
Madera strong in flowing Bowles,
Fill'd with extreme Delight our Souls;
'Till wearied with a purple Flood,
Of gen'rous Wine, the Giants Blood,
As Poets feign; away I made
For some refreshing verdant Shade;
Where musing on my Rambles strange,
And Fortune, which so oft did change,
In midst of various Contemplations,
Of Fancies odd and Meditations,
I slumber'd long, —
'Till airy Night and noxious Dews,
Did Sleep's unwholesome Fetters loose,
With Vapours cold and misty Air,
To Fire-side I did repair;

19. *Phaeton?*
20. Bed-bugs

Near which a jolly Female Crew,
Were deep engag'd at *Lanterloo*,[21]
In Nightrails white, with dirty Mien,
Such Sights are scarce in *England* seen:
I thought them first some Witches, bent
On black Designs, in dire Convent;
'Till one who with affected Air,
Had nicely learn'd to Curse and Swear,
Cry'd *Dealing's lost, 'tis but a Flam,*
And vow'd by *G*—*she'd have her Pam:*[22]
When Dealing thro' the Board had run,
They ask'd me kindly, *to make one:*
Not staying often to be bid,
I sate me down as others did;
We scarce had play'd a Round about,
But that those *Indian* Frows fell out:
D—*m you,* says one, *tho' now so Brave,*
I knew you late a Four Years Slave,
What, if for Planter's Wife you go,
Nature design'd you for the Hoe:
Rot you, replies the other streight,
The Captain kiss'd you for his Freight;
And if the Truth was known aright,
And how you walk'd the Streets by Night,
You'd blush, if one could blush for Shame,
Who from Bridewell *and* Newgate *came.*
From Words they fairly fell to Blows,
And being loth to interpose,
Or meddle in the Wars of Punk,
Away to Bed in Haste I slunk:
Waking next Day with aking Head,

21. The older form of a card game now called "Loo."
22. In Lanterloo or Loo the knave of clubs, called "Pam," was the highest card.

And Thirst that made me quit the Bed,
I rigg'd my self and soon got up,
To cool my Liver with a Cup
Of *Succahanah*[23] fresh and clear,
Not half so good as *English* Beer,
Which ready stood in Kitchin Pail,
And was, in Fact, but *Adam's* Ale.

FOR Planters Cellars, you must know,
Seldom with good *October* flow,
But Perry, Quince, and Apple Juice,
Spout from the Tap, like any Sluice,
Until the Cask grows low and stale,
They're forc'd again to Goard and Pail,
The soothing Draught scarce down my Throat,
Enough to set a Ship on float,
With *Cockerouse* as I was sitting
I felt a Fever intermitting,
A fiery Pulse beat in my Veins,
From cold I felt resembling Pains;
This cursed Seasoning I remember,
Lasted from *March* 'till cold *December;*
Nor could it then it's Quarter shift,
Until by *Carduus*[24] turn'd adrift:
And had my Doct'ress wanted Skill,
Or Kitchin-Phisick at her Will,
My Father's Son had lost his Lands,
And never seen the *Goodwin Sands:*[25]
But Thanks to *Fortune,* and a Nurse,
Whose Care depended on my Purse,

23. Sweet water.
24. Latin name for Thistle which, when dried and powdered, was mixed with water to reduce fevers.
25. A dangerous line of shoals about six miles off the coast of Kent, England.

[111]

I saw my self in good Condition,
Without the Help of a Physician:
At length the shivering Ill reliev'd
My Heart and Head, which long had griev'd.

I then began to think with Care,
How I might sell my *British* Ware;
That with my Freight I might comply,
Did on my Charter-Party lye:
To this Intent, with Guide before,
I tript it to the *Eastern* Shore;
Where riding near a Sandy Bay,
I met a Planter in my Way,
A pious, consciencious Rogue,
As e're wore Bonnet, Hat, or Brogue,
Who neither swore, nor kept his Word,
But cheated in the Fear o' th' Lord;
And when his Debts he could not pay,
From trusting Fools he'd run away.

WITH this sly Zealot, soon I struck
A Bargain, for my *English* Truck,
Agreeing for Ten Thousand Weight
Of *Sotweed* good, and fit for Freight:
Broad *Oronoko,* bright and sound,
The Growth and Product of his Ground;
In Cask, that shou'd contain compleat
Five Hundred of Tobacco neat.

THE Contract thus betwixt us made,
Not well acquainted with the Trade,
My Goods I trusted to the Cheat,
Whose Crop was then o'board the Fleet;

[112]

And going to receive my own,
I found the Bird was newly flown:
Cursing this execrable Slave,
This damn'd pretended Godly Knave,
On due Revenge and Justice bent,
I instantly to Council went;
Unto an ambodexter Quack,
Who learnedly had got the Knack
Of giving Clysters, making Pills,
Of filling Bonds, and forging Wills;
And with a Stock of Impudence,
Supply'd his want of Wit and Sence,
With Looks demure, amazing People,
No wiser than a Daw on Steeple:
My Anger flushing in my Face,
I stated the preceeding Case,
And of my Money was so free
That he'd have poison'd you or me,
And hang'd his Father on a Tree,
For such another tempting Fee.

SMILING, said he, the Cause is clear,
I'll manage him, you need not fear,
The Case is judg'd, good Sir, but look
In *Galen,* no, in my Lord *Cook,*
I vow to G—d, I was mistook:
I'll take out a Provincial Writ,
And trownce him for his knavish Wit,
Upon my Life, I'll win the Cause,
With as much Ease I cure the Yaws:
Resolv'd to plague the Holy Brother,
I set one Rogue to catch another.

[113]

TO try the Cause then fully bent,
Up to *Annapolis* I went,
A City situate on a Plain,
*Where scarce a House will keep out Rain;
The Buildings fram'd with Cypress rare,
Resembles much our *Southwark-Fair;*[26]
But Strangers there will scarcely meet,
With Market Place, Exchange, or Street;
And if the Truth I may report,
It's not so large as *Tottenham-Court.*[27]
St. Mary's[28] once was in Repute,
Now Here the Judges try the Suit,
And Lawyers twice a Year dispute.
As oft the Bench most gravely meet,
Some to get drink, and some to eat
A swinging Share of Country Treat:
But as for Justice write or wrong,
Not one amongst the numerous Throng
Knows what it means, or has the Heart,
To vindicate a Stranger's Part.

NOW, Court being call'd by beat of Drum,
The Judges left their Punch and Rum;
When Pettifogging Doctor draws
His Papers forth, and opens Cause;
And lest I should the Better get,
Brib'd Quack suppress'd his knavish Wit:

*This Account of Annapolis was given Twenty-Years ago, and does not resemble it's present State.

26. Across the Thames from London and known as the playground of Londoners.
27. Former municipal borough of the former county of Middlesex.
28. The original capital of colonial Maryland.

[114]

So Maid upon the Downy Field,
Pretends a Rape, and fights to yield:
The byass'd Court without Delay,
Adjudg'd my Debt in Country Pay,
In Pipe Staves, Corn, or Flesh of Boar,
Rare Cargo for the English Shore.
Raging with Grief, full Speed I ran,
To join the Fleet at *Kickatan:*[29]

(Ed. note: here follows Cook's first published version of the poem's conclusion—a version later regretted as too bitter by its author and replaced in subsequent editions.)

Embarqu'd and waiting for a Wind,
I left this dreadful Curse behind.
May Canniballs transported o'er the Sea
Prey on these slaves, as they have done on me;
May never Merchant's trading sails explore
This Cruel, this Inhospitable Shoar;
But left abandon'd by the World to starve,
May they sustain the Fate they well deserve:
May they turn Savage, or as *Indians* Wild,
From Trade, Converse, and Happiness exil'd;
Recreant to Heaven, may they adore the Sun,
And into Pagan Superstitions run
For Vengeance ripe————
May Wrath Divine then lay those Regions wast
Where no Man's* Faithful, nor Woman chast.

*The Author does not intend by this any of the English Gentlemen resident there.

29. Probably Kecoughtan, present-day Hampton, Virginia as this is a fine port, being at the confluence of the James, Nansemond, and Elizabeth rivers.

WILLIAM BYRD, II—WILDERNESS WIT

WILLIAM Byrd, II was born near the falls of the James River in Virginia. His father was one of a small group of middle-class immigrants whose determination, intrigues, and skill led them to the top of a self-made colonial aristocracy. William Byrd the younger was educated in England as befitted the "First Gentleman of Virginia." He studied law at the Middle Temple and was admitted to the bar in 1692, the year of his return to America. Elected to the House of Burgesses, Byrd returned to England in 1697 as an agent for the colony, but his father's death in 1704 forced another crossing to manage the family estate. Byrd represented the Old Dominion in England again from 1715 to 1726 at which time he came back to stay, building the gracious Westover as a monument to his own eminence.[1] His self-composed epitaph concludes:

> To all this were added a great elegance of taste and life.
> The well-bred gentleman and polite companion.
> The splendid economist and prudent father of a family.
> With the constant enemy of all exhorbitant power
> And hearty friend to the liberties of his country.[2]

Byrd, the second member of the family dynasty which still endures, served on the Governor's Council, but also defended the colonists against royal pressures and often found himself caught between the planters and English policy. Indeed, his life was an

1. Pierre Marambaud, *William Byrd of Westover, 1674–1744* (Charlottesville: University Press of Virginia, 1971).
2. Alden Hatch, *The Byrds of Virginia* (New York: Holt, Rinehart and Winston, 1969), p. 175.

attempt to combine the ethos of London with that of a distant agrarian colony. At the time of his death, he had amassed some 179,000 acres in Virginia, become a colonial political leader, managed the lives of hundreds of African slaves, and sought to manage his wife's periodic tantrums with cure-all "flourishes."[3]

In 1728, Byrd led an expedition which surveyed the Virginia-North Carolina boundary. He wrote a journal of his experiences and observations on this adventure but it was never published during his lifetime, circulating, instead, in manuscript form among his friends. While the record was filled with botanical observations and theories, one discovers that it retains its cohesion when edited for its humor alone. Byrd used punning, tall-tale exaggeration, ridicule, and satire for his comic effects. The uses to which he put these tricks are an accurate reflection of the man and his culture. As he put it, mirth was a means of turning "disasters into merriment," and a recurrent theme of the *Dividing Line* is the value of Laughter in wilderness survival. In mocking dangers, Byrd reaffirmed his cherished mastery as a civilized Englishman. Underneath the flippancies one senses the nervous apprehensions of a man trying to keep wild America at bay.

HISTORY OF THE DIVIDING LINE BETWIXT VIRGINA AND NORTH CAROLINA RUN IN THE YEAR OF OUR LORD 1728

Before I enter upon the journal of the line between Virginia and North Carolina, it will be necessary to clear the way to it by showing how the other British colonies on the main have, one after another, been carved out of Virginia by grants from His Majesty's royal predecessors. . . .

The first settlement of this fine country was owing to that great ornament of the British nation, Sir Walter Raleigh, who obtained a

---

3. Sexual intercourse, as in "I flourished her on the billiard table."

grant thereof from Queen Elizabeth, of ever-glorious memory, by letters patent dated March 25, 1584. . . .

They ventured ashore near that place upon an island now called Colleton Island, where they set up the arms of England and . . . made a very profitable voyage, raising at least a thousand per cent upon their cargo. Amongst other Indian commodities, they brought over some of that bewitching vegetable, tobacco. And this being the first that ever came to England, Sir Walter thought he could do no less than make a present of some of the brightest of it to his royal mistress for her own smoking. The Queen graciously accepted of it, but finding her stomach sicken after two or three whiffs, 'twas presently whispered by the Earl of Leicester's faction that Sir Walter had certainly poisoned her. But Her Majesty, soon recovering her disorder, obliged the Countess of Nottingham and all her maids to smoke a whole pipe out amongst them.

As it happened some ages before to be the fashion to saunter to the Holy Land and go upon other Quixote adventures, so it was now grown the humor to take a trip to America. . . . This modish frenzy, being still more inflamed by the charming account given of Virginia by the first adventurers, made many fond of removing to such a Paradise.

Happy was he, and still happier she, that could get themselves transported, fondly expecting their coarsest utensils in that happy place would be of massy silver.

This made it easy for the Company to procure as many volunteers as they wanted for their new colony, but like most other undertakers who have no assistance from the public, they starved the design by too much frugality; for, unwilling to launch out at first into too much expense, they shipped off but few people at a time, and those but scantily provided. The adventurers were, besides, idle and extravagant and expected they might live without work in so plentiful a country.

[The first settlers of the subsequent Virginia colony] . . . detested work more than famine. . . . They chose rather to depend upon musty provisions that were sent from England; and when they failed they were forced to take more pains to seek for wild fruits in the woods than they would have taken in tilling the ground. Besides, this exposed them to be knocked in the head by the Indians and gave them fluxes into the bargain, which thinned the plantation very much. To supply this mortality, they were reinforced the year following with a greater number of people, amongst which were fewer gentlemen and more laborers, who, however, took care not to kill themselves with work . . . they extended themselves as far as Jamestown, where, like true Englishmen, they built a church that cost no more than fifty pounds and a tavern that cost five-hundred.

They had now made peace with the Indians, but there was one thing wanting to make that peace lasting. The natives could by no means persuade themselves that the English were heartily their friends so long as they distained to intermarry with them. And, in earnest, had the English consulted their own security and the good of the colony, had they intended either to civilize or convert these gentiles, they would have brought their stomachs to embrace this prudent alliance.

The Indians are generally tall and well proportioned, which may make full amends for the darkness of their complexions. Add to this that they are healthy and strong, with constitutions untainted by lewdness and not enfeebled by luxury. Besides, morals and all considered, I cannot think the Indians were much greater heathens than the first adventurers, who, had they been good Christians, would have had the charity to take this only method of converting the natives to Christianity. For, after all that can be said, a sprightly lover is the most prevailing missionary that can be sent amongst these or any other infidels.

. . .

About the same time New England was pared off from Virginia . . . the first fourteen years this company encountered many difficulties and lost many men, though, far from being discouraged, they sent over numerous recruits of Presbyterians every year, who for all that had much ado to stand their ground, with all their fighting and praying.

But about the year 1620 a large swarm of dissenters fled thither from the severities of their stepmother, the church. These saints,

[119]

conceiving the same aversion to the copper complexion of the natives with that of the first adventurers to Virginia, would on no terms contract alliances with them, afraid, perhaps, like the Jews of old, lest they might be drawn into idolatry by those strange women. . . .

The proprietors of New Jersey, finding more trouble than profit in their new dominions, made over their right to several other persons, who obtained a fresh grant. . . .

Several of the grantees, being Quakers and Anabaptists, failed not to encourage many of their own persuasion to remove to this peaceful region. Amongst them were a swarm of Scots Quakers, who were not tolerated to exercise the gifts of the spirit in their own country.

Besides the hopes of being safe from persecution in this retreat, the new proprietors inveigled many over by this tempting account of the country: that it was a place free from those three great scourges of mankind, priests, lawyers, and physicians. Nor did they tell them a word of a lie, for the people were yet too poor to maintain these learned gentlemen, who everywhere love to be well paid for what they do and, like the Jews, can't breath in a climate where nothing is to be got. . . .

So soon as the bounds of New Jersey came to be distinctly laid off, it appeared there was still a narrow slip of land lying betwixt that colony and Maryland. Of this William Penn, a man of much worldly wisdom and some eminence among the Quakers, got early notice. . . .

It was a little surprising to some people how a Quaker should be so much in the graces of a popish prince, though, after all, it may be pretty well accounted for. This ingenious person had not been bred a Quaker but, in his early days, had been a man of pleasure about the town. He had a beautiful form and very taking address, which made him successful with the ladies, and particularly with a mistress of the Duke of Monmouth. By this gentlewoman he had a daughter, who had beauty enough to raise her to be a duchess and continued to be a toast full thirty years. But this amour had like to have brought our fine gentleman in danger of a duel, had he not discreetly sheltered himself under this peaceable persuasion. Besides, his father having been a flag officer in the navy while the Duke of York was Lord High Admiral might recommend the son to his favor. This piece of secret history I thought proper to mention to wipe off the suspicion of his having been popishly inclined.

. . .

The Quakers flocked over to this country in shoals, being adverse to go to Heaven the same way with the bishops. . . . The truth is, they have observed exact justice with all the natives that border upon them; they have purchased all their lands from the Indians, and though they paid but a trifle for them it has procured them the credit of being more righteous than their neighbors. They have likewise had the prudence to treat them kindly upon all occasions, which has saved them from many wars and massacres wherein the other colonies have been indiscreetly involved. The truth of it is, a people whose principles forbid them to draw the carnal sword were in the right to have no provocation.

[In 1663, the province of Carolina was created, but disputes immediately ensued as to the location of its northern border with Virginia. Byrd was named member of a delegation of Virginians who, with a group of counterparts from Carolina, were to survey an exact boundary line. The remainder of Byrd's *History* recounts his experiences in tracing the Virginia and North Carolina boundary through the wilderness.]

March 4, 1728: . . .

It was dark before we could reach the mouth of the river, where our wayward stars directed us to a miserable cottage. The landlord was lately removed bag and baggage from Maryland, through a strong antipathy he had to work and paying his debts. For want of our tent, we were obliged to shelter ourselves in this wretched hovel, where we were almost devoured by vermin of various kinds. However, we were above complaining, being all philosophers enough to improve such slender distresses into mirth and good humor.

[121]

5. The day being now come on which we had agreed to meet the commissioners of North Carolina, we embarked very early, which we could the easier do, having no temptation to stay where we were. . . . Farther still to the southward of us we . . . saw a small New England sloop riding in the sound a little to the south of our course. . . . The trade hither is engrossed by the saints of New England, who carry off a great deal of tobacco without troubling themselves with paying that impertinent duty of a penny a pound.

. . .

10. The only business here is raising of hogs, which is managed with the least trouble and affords the diet they are most fond of. The truth of it is, the inhabitants of North Carolina devour so much swine's flesh that it fills them full of gross humors. For want too, of a constant supply of salt, they are commonly obliged to eat it fresh, and that begets the highest taint of scurvy. Thus, whenever a severe cold happens to constitutions thus vitiated, 'tis apt to improve into the yaws, called there very justly the country distemper. . . . First, it seizes the throat, next the palate, and lastly shows its spite to the poor nose, of which 'tis apt in small time treacherously to undermine the foundation. . . . the disputes that happen about the beauty the noses have in some companies much ado to carry it. Nay, 'tis said that once, after three good pork years, a motion had like to have been made in the House of Burgesses that a man with a nose should be incapable of holding any place of profit in the province; which extraordinary motion could never have been intended without some hopes of a majority.

15. . . . the distemper of laziness seizes the men oftener much than the women. These last spin, weave, and knit, all with their own hands, while their husbands, depending on the bounty of the climate, are slothful in everything but getting of children, and in that only instance make themselves useful members of an infant colony.

17. . . . One thing may be said for the inhabitants of that province, that they are not troubled with any religious fumes and have the least superstition of any people living. They do not know

Sunday from any other day, any more than Robinson Crusoe did, which would give them a great advantage were they given to be industrious. But they keep so many Sabbaths every week that their disregard of the seventh day has no manner of cruelty in it, either to servants or cattle.

19. . . . In the meantime, whole flocks of women and children flew hither to stare at us with as much curiosity as if we had lately landed from Bantam[4] or Morocco. Some borderers, too, had a great mind to know where the line would come out, being for the most part apprehensive lest their lands should be taken into Virginia. In that case, they must have submitted to some sort of order and government; whereas, in North Carolina, everyone does what seems best in his own eyes. There were some good women that brought their children to be baptized, but brought no capons along with them to make the solemnity cheerful. In the meantime, it was strange that none came to be married in such a multitude, if it had only been for the novelty of having hands joined by one in holy orders. Yet so it was that though our chaplain christened above an hundred, he did not marry so much as one couple during the whole expedition. But marriage is reckoned a lay contract in Carolina, as I said before, and a country justice can tie the fatal knot there as fast as an archbishop. . . .

20. It was now a great misfortune to the men to find their provisions grow less as their labor grew greater; they were all forced to come to short allowance and consequently to work hard without filling their bellies. Though this was very severe upon English stomachs, yet the people were so far from being discomfited at it that they still kept up their good humor and merrily told a young fellow in the company, who looked very plump and wholesome, that he must expect to go first to pot if matters should come to extremity. This was only said by way of jest, yet it made him thoughtful in earnest. However, for the present he returned them a very civil answer, letting them know that, dead or alive, he should be glad to be useful to such worthy good friends. But, after all, this

4. Northwest Java.

[123]

humerous saying had one very good effect, for that younker,[5] who before was a little inclined by his constitution to be lazy, grew on a sudden extremely industrious, that so there might be less occasion to carbonade[6] him for the good of his fellow travelers.

25. . . . Surely there is no place in the world where the inhabitants live with less labor than in North Carolina. It approaches nearer to the description of Lubberland[7] than any other, by the great felicity of the climate, the easiness of raising provisions, and the slothfulness of the people. . . . The men, for their parts, just like the Indians, impose all the work upon the poor women. They make their wives rise out of their beds early in the morning, at the same time that they lie and snore till the sun has risen one-third of his course and dispersed all the unwholesome damps. Then, after stretching and yawning for half an hour, they light their pipes, and, under the protection of a cloud of smoke, venture out into the open air; though if it happen to be never so little cold they quickly return shivering into the chimney corner. When the weather is mild, they stand leaning with both their arms upon the cornfield fence and gravely consider whether they had best go and take a small heat at the hoe but generally find reasons to put it off till another time. . . . To speak the truth, 'tis a thorough aversion to labor that makes people file off to North Carolina, where plenty and a warm sun confirm them in their disposition to laziness for their whole lives.

27. . . . Edenton . . . is situate on the north side of Albemarle Sound . . . A dirty slash[8] runs all along the back of it, which in the summer is a foul annoyance and furnishes abundance of that Carolina plague, mosquitoes. There may be forty or fifty houses, most of them small and built without expense. A citizen here is counted extravagant if he has ambition enough to aspire to a brick chimney. Justice herself is but indifferently lodged, the courthouse having much the air of a common tobacco house. I believe this is

5. Youngster.
6. Broil over hot coals.
7. An imaginary land of plenty without labor.
8. A low, swampy marsh.

the only metropolis in the Christian or Mahometan world where there is neither church, chapel, mosque, synagogue, or any other place of public worship of any sect or religion whatsoever. What little devotion there may happen to be is much more private than their vices. The people seem easy without a minister as long as they are exempted from paying him. Sometimes the Society for Propagating the Gospel[9] has had the charity to send over missionaries to this country; but, unfortunately, the priest has been too lewd for the people, or, which oftener happens, they too lewd for the priest. For these reasons these reverend gentlemen have always left their flocks as arrant heathen as they found them. This much, however, may be said for the inhabitants of Edenton, that not a soul has the least taint of hypocrisy or superstition, acting very frankly and aboveboard in all their exercises.

April 20. . . . Mr. Kinchen had unadvisedly sold the men a little brandy of his own making, which produced much disorder, causing some to be too choleric and others too loving; insomuch that a damsel who assisted in the kitchen had certainly suffered what the nuns call martyrdom had she not capitulated a little too soon. This outrage would have called for some severe discipline, had she not bashfully withdrawn herself early in the morning and so carried off the evidence.

October 6. . . . In the afternoon, Mr. Fitzwilliam, one of the commissioners for Virginia, acquainted his collegues it was his opinion that by His Majesty's order they could not proceed farther on the line but in conjunction with the commissioners of Carolina [who had decided to return homeward, much to Byrd's irritation]; for which reason he intended to retire the next morning with those gentlemen. This looked a little odd in our brother commissioner; though, in justice to him as well as to our Carolina friends, they stuck by us as long as our good liquor lasted and were so kind to us as to drink our good journey to the mountains in the last bottle we had left.

October 7. . . . We had now no other drink but what Adam drank in Paradise, though to our comfort we found the water

9. The missionary arm of the Church of England.

[125]

excellent, by the help of which we perceived our appetites to mend, our slumbers to sweeten, the stream of life to run cool and peaceably in our veins, and if ever we dreamt of women, they were kind.

October 14. . . . As I sat in the tent, I overheard a learned conversation between one of our men and the Indian. He ask[ed] the Englishman what it was that made that rumbling noise when it thundered. The man told him merrily that the God of the English was firing his great guns upon the god of the Indians, which made all that roaring in the clouds, and that the lightening was only the flash of those guns. The Indian, carrying on the humor, replied very gravely he believed that might be the case indeed, and that the rain which followed upon the thunder must be occasioned by the Indian god's being so scared he could not hold his water.

October 19. . . . About four miles beyond the river Irvin we forded Matrimony Creek, called so by an unfortunate married man because it was exceedingly noisy and impetuous. However, though the stream was clamorous, yet like those women who make themselves plainest heard, it was likewise perfectly clear and unsullied.

October 30. . . . This being His Majesty's birthday, we drank all the loyal healths in excellent water, not for the sake of the drink (like many of our fellow subjects), but purely for the sake of the toast. And because all public mirth should be a little noisy, we fired several volleys of canes, instead of guns, which gave a loud report. We threw them into the fire, where the air enclosed betwixt the joints of the canes, being expanded by the violent heat, burst its narrow bounds with a considerable explosion.

October 31. . . . Our hunters killed a large doe and two bears, which made all other misfortunes easy. Certainly no Tartar ever loved horseflesh or Hottentot guts and garbage better than woodsmen do bear. The truth of it is, it may be proper food perhaps for such as work or ride it off, but, with our chaplain's leave, who loved it much, I think it not a very proper diet for saints, because 'tis apt to make them a little too rampant. And, now, for the good of mankind and for the better peopling an infant colony, which has no want but that of inhabitants, I will venture to publish a secret of importance which our Indian disclosed to me. I asked him the

[126]

reason why few or none of his countrywomen were barren. To which curious question he answered, with a broad grin upon his face, they had an infallible secret for that. Upon my being importunate to know what the secret might be, he informed me that if any Indian woman did not prove with child at a decent time after marriage, the husband, to save his reputation with the women, forthwith entered into a bear diet for six weeks, which in that time makes him so vigorous that he grows exceedingly impertinent to his poor wife, and 'tis great odds but he makes her a mother in nine months. And thus much I am able to say besides for the reputation of the bear diet, that all the married men of our company were joyful fathers within forty weeks after they got home, and most of the single men had children sworn to them within the same time, our chaplain always excepted, who, with much ado, made a shift to cast out that importunate kind of devil by dint of fasting and prayer.

November 4. . . . One of the young fellows we had sent to bring up the tired horses entertained us in the evening with a remarkable adventure he had met with that day. He had straggled, it seems, from his company in a mist and made a cub of a year old betake itself to a tree. While he was new-priming his piece with intent to fetch it down, the old gentlewoman appeared and, perceiving her heir apparent in distress, advanced open-mouthed to his relief. The man was so intent upon his game that she had approached very near him before he perceived her. But finding his danger, he faced about upon the enemy, which immediately reared upon her posteriors and put herself in battle array. The man, admiring at the bear's assurance, endeavored to fire upon her, but by the dampness of the priming his gun did not go off. He cocked it a second time and had the same misfortune. After missing fire twice, he had the folly to punch the beast with the muzzle of his piece; but Mother Bruin, being upon her guard, seized the weapon with her paws and by main strength wrenched it out of the fellow's hands. The man, being thus fairly disarmed, thought himself no longer a match for the enemy and therefore retreated as fast as his legs could carry him. The brute naturally grew bolder upon the flight of her adversary and pursued him with all her heavy speed.

[127]

For some time it was doubtful whether fear made one run faster or fury the other. But after an even course of about fifty yards, the man had the mishap to stumble over a stump and fell down at his full length. He now would have sold his life a pennyworth; but the bear, apprehending there might be some trick in the fall, instantly halted and looked with much attention on her prostrate foe. In the meanwhile, the man had with great presence of mind resolved to make the bear believe he was dead by lying breathless on the ground, in hopes that the beast would be too generous to kill him over again. To carry on the farce, he acted the corpse for some time without daring to raise his head to see how near the monster was to him. But in about two minutes, to his unspeakable comfort, he was raised from the dead by the barking of a dog belonging to one of his companions, who came seasonably to his rescue and drove the bear from pursuing the man to take care of her cub, which she feared might now fall into a second distress.

November 12. . . . Our hunters shot nothing this whole day but a straggling bear, which happened to fall by the hand of the very person who had been lately disarmed and put to flight, for which he declared war against the whole species.

November 14. . . . One of our people shot a large grey squirrel with a very bushy tail, a singular use of which our merry Indian discovered to us. He said whenever this little animal has occasion to cross a run of water, he launches a chip or piece of bark into the water on which he embarks and, holding up his tail to the wind, sails over very safely. If this be true, 'tis probable men learnt at first the use of sails from these ingenious little animals, as the Hottentots learnt the physical use of most of their plants from the baboons.

November 17. This being Sunday, we were seasonably' put in mind how much we were obliged to be thankful for our happy return to the inhabitants. . . . As for the misadventures of sticking in the mire and falling into rivers and creeks, they were rather subjects of mirth than complaint and served only to diversify our travels with a little farcical variety.

November 18. . . . All the grandees of the Samponi nation did us the honor to repair hither to meet us, and our worthy friend and

[128]

fellow traveler, Bearskin, appeared among the gravest of them in his robes of ceremony. Four young ladies of the first quality came with them, who had more the air of cleanliness than any copper-colored beauties I had ever seen;[10] yet we resisted all their charms, notwithstanding the long fast we had kept from the sex and the bear diet we had been so long engaged in. Nor can I say the price they set upon their charms was at all exorbitant. A princess for a pair of red stockings can't, surely, be thought buying repentance much too dear.

. . . All Indians have as great an aversion to hanging as the Muscovites, though perhaps not for the same cleanly reason, these last believing that the soul of one that dies in this manner, being forced to sally out of the body at the postern, must needs be defiled.

. . .

The most uncommon circumstance in this Indian visit was that they all come on horseback, . . . The men rode more awkwardly than any Dutch sailor, and the ladies bestrode their palfreys *a la mode de France* but were so bashful about it that there was no persuading them to mount till they were quite out of our sight. The French women use to ride astraddle, not so much to make them sit firmer in the saddle as from the hopes that same thing might peradventure befall them that once happened to the nun of Orleans, who, escaping out of nunnery, took post *en cavalier* and in ten miles' hard riding had the good fortune to have all the tokens of a man break out upon her.[11]

November 19. . . . About eight miles farther we came to Sturgeon Creek, so called from the dexterity an Occaneechi Indian showed there in catching one of those royal fish, which was performed after the following manner; in the summertime 'tis no unusual thing for sturgeons to sleep on the surface of the water, and one of them, having wandered up into this creek in the spring, was

10. For all his strong feelings about Indian-white intermarriage, Byrd was offended by the Indian practice of covering the body with bear's grease to ward off bugs. This, when combined with grime, produced a bodily patina.

11. Until it was decided that women were human and had souls, the only hope of escaping servitude or the convent was in becoming a man.

floating in that drowsy condition. The Indian above-mentioned ran up to the neck into the creek a little below the place where he discovered the fish, expecting the stream would soon bring his game down to him. He judged the matter right, and as soon as it came within his reach, he whipped a running noose over his jowl. This waked the sturgeon, which, being strong in its own element, darted immediately under water and dragged the Indian after him. The man made it a point of honor to keep his hold, which he did to the apparent danger of being drowned. Sometimes both the Indian and the fish disappeared for a quarter of a minute and then rose at some distance from where they dived. At this rate they continued flouncing about, sometimes above and sometimes under water, for a considerable time, till at last the hero suffocated his adversary and haled his body ashore in triumph.

. . . We had but two miles more to Captain Embry's, where we found the housekeeping much better than the house. Our bountiful landlady had set her oven and all her spits, pots, gridirons, and saucepans to work to diversify our entertainment, though after all it proved but a Mahometan feast, there being nothing to drink but water. The worst of it was we had unluckily outrid the baggage and for that reason were obliged to lodge very sociably in the same apartment with the family, where, reckoning women and children, we mustered in all no less than nine persons, who all pigged lovingly together.

November 20. . . . At the end of thirty good miles, we arrived at Colonel Bolling's, where first from a primitive course of life we began to relapse into luxury. . . . While the commissioners fared sumptuously here, the poor chaplain and two surveyors stopped ten miles short at a poor planter's house in pity to their horses, where they made a St. Anthony's meal,[12] that is, they supped upon the pickings of what stuck in their teeth ever since breakfast. But to make them amends, the good man laid them in his own bed, where they all three nestled together in one cotton sheet and one of brown

12. The disease now called "Shingles" was referred to then as "St. Anthony's Fire." Relief called for a water diet.

Osnaburgs, made still something browner by two month's copious perspiration.

But those worthy gentlemen were so alert in the morning after their light supper that they came up with us before breakfast and honestly paid their stomachs all they owed them.

November 22. A little before noon we all took leave and dispersed to our several habitations, where we were so happy as to find all our families well. This crowned all our other blessings and made our journey as prosperous as it had been painful. . . .

"UPON A FART"[13]
William Byrd, II

Gentlest Blast of ill concoction,
Reverse of high-ascending Belch:
Th' only Stink abhorr'd by Scotsman,
Belovd and practic'd by the Welch.

Softest noat of Inward Gripeing
Sr Reverences finest part,
So fine it needs no pains of Wipeing,
Except it prove a Brewers fart.

Swiftest Ease of Cholique pain,
Vapor from a Secret Stench,
Is rattled out by th' unbred Swain,
But whispered by the Bashfull wench.

Shapeless Fart! we ne'er can show Thee
But in that merry Female Sport
In which by burning blew we know Thee
Th' Amuzement of the Maids at Court.

13. Kenneth Silverman, ed., *Colonial American Poetry* (New York: Anchor Books, 1968), pp. 273–74.

THE ITINERARIUM

OF DR. ALEXANDER HAMILTON

[1744]

THE author of this delightful travel diary was no relation to the more famous "Founding Father" and Secretary of the Treasury under President Washington. This *Itinerarium* was the work of Dr. Alexander Hamilton, who was born at or near Edinburgh, Scotland in 1712.[1] His father was Professor of Divinity and Principal of the University of Edinburgh and his family held a recognized place in the Scottish gentry.

The young Hamilton went to medical school at the university and was granted the degree of Doctor of Medicine in 1737. His brother John, a minister, migrated to Maryland and Alexander followed him in 1739, settling in Annapolis. Given his extensive university education, his profession, and his family name, Alexander Hamilton was welcomed by the local gentry as one of theirs and went on to marry the daughter of the richest and most powerful family in the colony.

What distinguished Dr. Hamilton then and now was his acutely fine, if haughty, sense of humor and his unerring eye for the manners and customs of his contemporaries. The two are thoroughly blended in his *Itinerarium* of a long journey he made from Annapolis to York, Maine and back again in 1744. The good doctor was suffering from a dangerous pulmonary condition and prescribed himself a challenging and refreshing vacation. Happily, he kept a record of what he saw and those whom he encountered.

The journal reveals a man who joined his strong sense of humor

1. Carl Bridenbaugh, ed., *Gentleman's Progress, the Itinerarium of Dr. Alexander Hamilton 1744,* (Chapel Hill, N.C.: University of North Carolina Press for the Institute of Early American History and Culture, 1948), p. xii.

to his very definite ideas of correct behavior and social distinctions. Like Mrs. Knight and Robert Hunter, Hamilton was beset by a parade of intrusive, pretentious, and often unsavory types who were bold enough to question his presence. As he travelled in fine clothes and was accompanied by a slave, he must have cut an impressive figure. Still, unsolicited questions were not to be tolerated by the gentry, and a biting sarcasm kept the bumpkins at bay. If the dogs were bent upon playing democratic games, Hamilton forced them to withstand his withering disapproval.

Of all the humorists whose words have survived, Alexander Hamilton best depicts everyday social intercourse in the wilderness. In the many taverns, roominghouses, and coffeeshops he visited he constructed a lively tableau of the wide variety of characters who enlivened the wilderness.

W.H.K.

Annapolis, Wednesday, May 30th. [1744] I set out from Annapolis in Maryland . . . I put up att one Tradaway's about 10 miles from Joppa. . . . Just as I dismounted att Tradaway's, I found a drunken club dismissing. Most of them had got upon their horses and were seated in an oblique situation, deviating much from a perpendicular to the horizontal plan(e), a posture quite necessary for keeping the center of gravity within its proper base for the support of the superstructure; hence we deduce the true physicall reason why our heads overloaded with liquor become too ponderous for our heels. Their discourse was as oblique as their position; the only thing intelligible in it was oaths and God dammes; the rest was an inarticulate sound like Rabelais' frozen words a thawing, interlaced with hickupings and belchings. I was uneasy till they were gone, and my landlord, seeing me stare, made that trite apology—that indeed he did not care to have such disorderly fellows come about his house; he was always noted far and near for keeping a quiet house and entertaining only gentlemen or such like, but these were country people, his neighbours, and it was not prudent to dissoblige them upon slight occasions. "Alas, sir!"

added he, "we that entertain travellers must strive to oblige every body, for it is our dayly bread." While he spoke thus, our Bacchanalians, finding no more rum in play, rid off helter skelter as if the devil had possessed them, every man sitting his horse in a see-saw manner like a bunch of rags tyed upon the saddle.

I found nothing particular or worth notice in my landlord's character or conversation, only as to his bodily make. He was a fat pursy man and had large bubbies like a woman. I supped upon fry'd chickens and bacon, and after supper the conversation turned upon politicks, news, and the dreaded French war; but it was so very lumpish and heavy that it disposed me mightily to sleep. This learned company consisted of the landlord, his overseer and miller, and another greasy thumb'd fellow who, as I understood, professed physick and particular surgery. In the drawing of teeth, he practiced upon the house maid, a dirty piece of lumber, who made such screaming and squalling as made me imagine there was murder going forwards in the house. However, the artist got the tooth out att last with a great clumsy pair of blacksmith's forceps; and indeed it seemed to require such an instrument, for when he showed it to us, it resembled a horsenail more than a tooth.

. . .

Narrows Ferry

I came to the Narrows att two a'clock and dined att one Corson's that keeps the ferry. The landlady spoke both Dutch and English. I dined upon what I had never eat in my life before—a dish of fryed clams, of which shell fish there is abundance in these parts. As I sat down to dinner I observed a manner of saying grace quite new to me. My landlady and her two daughters put on solemn, devout faces, hanging down their heads and holding up their hands for half a minute. I, who had gracelessly fallen too without remembering that duty according to a wicked custom I had contracted, sat staring att them with my mouth choak full, but after this short meditation was over, we began to lay about us and stuff down the fryed clams with rye-bread and butter. They took such a deal of chawing that we were long att dinner, and the dish began to cool before we had eat enough. The landlady called for the bedpan. I could not guess what she intended to do with it unless it was to warm her bed to go to sleep after dinner, but I found that it was used by way of a chaffing dish to warm our dish of clams. I stared att the novelty for some time, and reaching over for a mug of beer that stood on the opposite side of the table, my bag sleeve catched hold of the handle of the bed pan and unfortunately overset the clams, at which the landlady was a little ruffled and muttered a scrape of Dutch of which I understood not a word. . . .

Schenectady

Saturday, June 30 . . . Att ten o'clock M————s and I went to the island, where we dined, and M————s, being hot with walking, went to drink his cool water as usuall which brought an ague upon him, and he was obliged to go to bed. In the mean time the old woman and I conversed for a half an hour about a rurall life and good husbandry. Att three o'clock I walked abroad to view the island, and sitting under a willow near the water, I was invited to sleep, but scarce had I enjoyed half an hour's repose when I was waked by a cow that was eating up my handkercheff which I had put under my head. I pursued her for some time before I recovered it, when I supposed the snuff in it made her disgorge, but it was prittily pinked all over with holes. . . .

Nutting Island

Friday, June 22d. (1744) . . . Early this morning two passengers came on board of the sloop, a man and a woman, both Dutch. The man was named Marcus Van Bummill. He came on board drunk and gave us a surfet of bad English. If any body laughed when he spoke, he was angry, being jealous that they thought him a fool. He had a good deal of the bully and braggadocio in him, but when thwarted or threatened, he seemed faint hearted and cowardly. Understanding that I was a valitudinarian, he began to advise me how to manage my constitution. "You drink and whore

[135]

too much," said he, "and that makes you thin and sickly. Could you abstain as I have done and drink nothing but water for 6 weeks, and have to do with no women but your own lawfull wife, your belly and cheeks would be like mine, look ye, plump and smooth and round." With that he clapt his hands upon his belly and blowd up his cheeks like a trumpeter. He brought on board with him a runlett[2] of rum, and, taking it into his head that somebody had robed him of a part of it, he went down into the hold and fell a swearing bitterly by *Dunder Sacramentum,* and *Jesu Christus.* I, being upon deck and hearing a strange noise below, looked down and saw him expanding his hands and turning up his eyes as if he had been at prayers. He was for having us all before a magistrate about it, but att last Knockson, the master of the sloop, swore him into good humour again and perswaded him that his rum was all safe. He quoted a deal of scripture, but his favorite topics when upon that subject was about King David, and King Solomon, and the shape and size of the Tower of Babel. He pretended to have been mighty familiar with great folks when they came in his way, and this familiarity of his was so great as even to scorn and contemn them to their faces. After a deal of talk and rattle, he went down and slept for four hours and, when he waked, imagined he had slept a whole day and a night, swearing it was Saturday night when it was only Friday afternoon. There was a Dutch woman on board, remarkably ugly, upon whom this Van Bummill cast a loving eye and wanted much to be att close conference with her. . . .

New York

Friday, July 6th. . . . I went to the inn to see my horses, and finding them in good plight, Mr. Waghorn desired me to walk into a room where were some Boston gentlemen that would be company for me in my journey there. I agreed to set out with them for Boston upon Monday morning. Their names were Messrs. Laughton and Parker, by employment traders. There was in company an old grave don who, they told me, was both a parson and physitian. Being a graduate, he appeared to be in a mean attire. His wig was

2. A small barrel or cask of volume equal to eighteen wine gallons.

remarkably weather beaten, the hairs being all as streight as a rush and of an orange yellow at the extremitys, but that it had been once a fair wig you might know by the appearance of that part which is covered by the hat, for that head wear, I suppose, seldom went off unless att propper times to yield place to his night cap. The uncovered part of his wig had changed its huc by the sun beams and rain alternatly beating upon it. This old philosopher had besides, as part of his wearing aparrell, a pair of old greasy gloves not a whit less ancient than the wig, which lay carefully folded up upon the table before him. And upon his legs were a pair of old leather spatterdashes, clouted in twenty different places and buttoned up all along the outside of his leg with brass buttons. He was consumedly grave and sparing of his talk, but every now and then a dry joke escaped him.

Att the opposite side of the table sat another piece of antiquity, one Major Spratt, a thin, tall man, very phtisicall [phthisical, i.e. tubercular] and addicted much to a dry cough. His face was adorned and set out with very large carbuncles, and he was more than half seas over in liquor. I understood he professed poetry and often applied himself to rhiming, in which he imagined himself a very good artist. He gave us a specimen of his poetry in an epitaph which he said he had composed upon one Purcell, a neighbour of his, lately dead; asked us if we did not think it excellent and the best of that kind ever we heard. He repeated it ten times over with a ludicrous air and action. "Gentlemen," said he, "pray take notise now, give good attention. It is perhaps the concisest, wittiest, prittiest epigram or epitaph, call it what you will, that you ever heard. Shall I get you pen and ink to write it down? Perhaps you mayn't remember it else. It is highly worth your noting. Pray observe how it runs,—

> Here lyes John Purcell;
> And whether he be in heaven or in hell,
> Never a one of us all can tell.

This poet asked me very kindly how I did and took me by the hand,

[137]

tho I never had seen him in my life before. He said he liked me for the sake of my name, told me he was himself nearly related to Coll. Hamilton in the Jerseys, son of the late Govr. Hamilton there.[3] Then from one digression to another he told me that the coat he had upon his back was 30 years old. I believed him, for every button was as large as an ordinary turnip, the button holes att least a quarter of a yard long, and the pocket holes just down att the skirts.

After some confused topsy turvy conversation, the landlord sung a bawdy song att which the grave parson-doctor got up, told us that was a language he did not understand, and therefore took his horse and rid away; but in little more than half an hour or three quarters returned again and told us he had forgot his gloves and had rid two miles of his way before he missed them. I was surprized at the old man's care of such a greasy bargain as these gloves. They were fit for nothing but to be wore by itchified persons under a course of sulphur, and I don't know but the doctor had lent them to some of his patients for that purpose, by which means they had imbibed such a quantity of grease. The landlord told me he was a man worth 5000 pounds sterl. and had got it by frugality. I replied that this instance of the gloves was such a demonstration of carefullness that I wondered he was not worth twice as much.

At four a'clock I came to my lodging and drank tea with Mrs. Hog, and Mr. John Watts, a Scots gentleman, came to pay me a visit. Att 5 I went to the coffee house, and there meeting with Mr. Dupeyster, he carried me to the taveren where in a large room was conveen'd a certain club of merry fellows. Among the rest was H———d, the same whom I extolled before for his art in touching the violin, but that indeed seemed to be his principall excellency. Other things he pretended to but fell short. He affected being a witt and dealt much in pointed satyre, but it was such base metall that the edge or point was soon turned when put to the proof. When any body spoke to him, he seemed to give ear in such a careless manner as if he thought all discourse but his own triffling and insignificant. In short he was fit to shine no where but among your good natured

3. Another Andrew Hamilton (d. 1703) who was governor of New Jersey from 1699 to 1702.

men and ignorant blockheads. There was a necessity for the first to bear with the stupidity of his satire and for the others to admire his pseudosophia and quaintness of his speeches and, att the same time, with their blocks, to turn the edge and acuteness of his wit. He dealt much in proverbs and made use of one which I thought pritty significant when well applied. It was *the devil to pay and no pitch hot?* An interrogatory adage metaphorically derived from the manner of sailors who pay their ship's bottoms with pitch. I back'd it with *great cry and little wool, said the devil when he shore his hogs,* applicable enough to the ostentation and clutter he made with his learning.

There was in this company one Dr. McGraa, a pretended Scots-man, but by brogue a Teague.[4] He had an affected way of curtsieing instead of bowing when he entered a room. He put on a modest look uncommon to his nation, spoke little, and when he went to speak, leaned over the table and streeched out his neck and face, goose-like, as if he had been going to whisper you in the ear. When he drank to any in the company, he would speak but kept bowing and bowing, sometimes for the space of a minute or two, till the person complimented either observed him of his own accord or was hunched into attention by his next neighbour; but it was hard to know who he bowed to upon account of his squinting. However, when the liquor began to heat him a little, he talked at the rate of three words in a minute, and sitting next me (he was very complaisant in his cups), he told me he had heard my name mentioned by some Marylanders and asked me if I knew his unkle Grierson in Maryland. I returned his compliments in as civil a manner as possible, and for half an hour we talked of nothing but waiting upon one another at our lodgings, but after all this complimentary farce and promises of serving and waiting was over, I could not but observe that none of us took the trouble to enquire where the one or the other lodged. I never met with a man so wrapt up in himself as this fellow seemed to be, nor did I ever see a face where there was so much effronterie under a pretended mask of modesty.

There was, besides, another doctor in company named Man, a

4. English nickname for an Irishman.

doctor of a man of war. The best thing I saw about him was that he would drink nothing but water, but he eat lustily at supper, and nothing remarkable appeared in his discourse (which indeed was copious and insipid) but only an affected way he had of swearing by Ged att every two words; and by the motion of his hands at each time of swearing that polite and elegant oath, he would seem to let the company understand that he was no mean orator, and that the little oath was a very fine ornament to his oration.

But the most remarkable person in the whole company was one Wendal, a young gentleman from Boston. He entertained us mightily by playing on the violin the quickest tunes upon the highest keys, which he accompanied with his voice so as even to drown the violin with such nice shakings and gracings that I thought his voice outdid the instrument. I sat for some time imoveable with surprize. The like I never heard, and the thing seemed to me next a miracle. The extent of his voice is impossible to describe or even to imagine unless by hearing him. The whole company were amazed that any person but a woman or eunuch could have such a pipe and began to question his virility; but he swore that if the company pleased he would show a couple of as good witnesses as any man might wear. He then imitated severall beasts, as cats, dogs, horses, and cows, with the cackling of poultry, and all to such perfection that nothing but nature could match it. When the landlord (a clumsy, tallow faced fellow in a white jacket) came to receive his reckoning, our mimick's art struck and surprized him in such a manner that it fixed him quite, like one that had seen the Gorgon's head, and he might have passed for a statue done in white marble. He was so struck that the company might have gone away without paying and carried off all his silver tankards and spoons, and he never would have observed.

After being thus entertained I returned to my lodging att 11 o'clock. . . .

Salem Ferry—Ipswich

Tuesday, July 31. At eleven o'clock this morning Mr. Malcolm accompanied me to Salem Ferry where I crossed and rid a pleasant levell road all the way to Ipswich, where the houses are so thick planted that it looks like one continued village. I put up at one Howel's in Ipswich att the Sign of the Armed Knight. I waited upon Mr. John Rogers, the minister there, and delivered him a paquet of letters from his son att Annapolis. I returned again to the taveren and there met a talkative old fellow who was very inquisitive about my place of abode and occupation, as he called it. He frequently accosted me with *please your honour,* with which grand title, like some fools whom I know, I seemed highly pleased tho I was conscious it did not belong to me. When I told him I came from Maryland, he said he had frequently read of that place but never had seen it. This old fellow, by his own account, had read of every thing but had seen nothing. He affected being a schollar, or a man much given to reading or study, and used a great many hard words in discourse, which he generally missapplied.

There was likewise a young man in company who rid with me some miles on my way to Newberry. He valued himself much upon the goodness of his horse and said that he was a prime beast as ever went upon 4 legs or wore hoofs. He told me he had a curiosity to ride to Maryland but was afraid of the terrible woods in the way and asked me if there were not a great many dangerous wild beasts in these woods. I told him that the most dangerous wild beasts in these woods were shaped exactly like men, and they went by the name of buckskins, or bucks, tho they were not bucks neither but some-thing, as it were, betwixt a man and a beast. "Bless us! You don't say so," says he; "then surely you had needs ride with guns" (meaning my pistols). I parted with this wiseacre when I had got about half way to Newbury.

A little farther I met a fat sheep driving in a chaise, a negroe sitting upon the box. I asked the negroe if that was his master. He told me no, but that it was a weather belonging to Mr. Jones, who had strayed and would not come home without being carried. Passing by this prodigy I met another, which was two great fat women riding upon one horse. . . .

Newburry Ferry—Hampton

Wednesday, August 1. This morning proved very rainy, and there-

[141]

for I did not set out till eleven o'clock. I crossed Newburry Ferry and rid a pleasant even road, only somewhat stonny, and in a perpetual drizzle so that I could not have an advantageous view of the country round me. Att half an hour after one I passed thro Hampton, a very long, scattered town.

Having proceeded some miles farther I was overtaken by a man who bore me company all the way to Portsmouth. He was very inquisitive about where I was going, whence I came, and who I was. His questions were all stated in the rustick civil stile. "Pray sir, if I may be so bold, where are you going?" "Prithee, friend," says I, "where are you going?" "Why, I go along the road here a little way." "So do I, friend," replied I. "But may I presume, sir, whence do you come?" "And from whence do you come, friend?" says I. "Pardon me, from John Singleton's farm," replied he, "with a bag of oats." "And I come from Maryland," said I, "with a portmanteau and baggage." "Maryland!" said my companion, "where the devil is that there place? I have never heard of it. But pray, sir, may I be so free as to ask your name?" "And may I be so bold as to ask yours, friend?" said I. "Mine is Jerry Jacobs, att your service," replied he. I told him that mine was Bombast Huynhym van Helmont, att his service. "A strange name indeed; belike your a Dutchman, sir,—a captain of a ship, belike." "No, friend," says I, "I am a High German alchymist." "Bless us! You don't say so; that's a trade I never heard of; what may you deal in sir?" "I sell air," said I. "Air," said he, "damn it, a strange commodity. I'd thank you for some wholsom air to cure my fevers which have held me these two months." I have noted down this dialogue as a specimen of many of the same tenour I had in my journey when I met with these inquisitive rusticks. . . .

Boston

I left my horses at Barker's stables and drank tea with my landlady, Mrs. Guneau. There was in the company a pritty young lady. The character of a certain Church of England clergiman in Boston was canvassed, he having lost his living for being too sweet upon his landlady's daughter, a great belly being the consequence. I pitied him only for his imprudence and want of policy. As for the crime, considdered in a certain light it is but a peccadillo, and he might have escaped unobserved had he had the same cunning as some others of his brethren who doubtless are as deep in the dirt as he in the mire. I shall not mention the unfortunate man's name (absit foeda calumnia),[5] but I much commiserated his calamity and regretted the loss, for he was an excellent preacher; but the wisest men have been led into silly scrapes by the attractions of that vain sex, which, I think, explains a certain enigmatic verse

> Diceti grammatici, cur mascula nomina cunnus
> Et cur Famineum mentula nomen habet[6]

The first is masculine, because it attracts the male, the latter feminine, because it is an effeminate follower of the other.

I had the opportunity this night of seeing Mons. la Moinnerie, my fellow lodger. He was obliged to keep the house close for fear of being made a prisoner of war. He was the strangest mortal for eating ever I knew. He would not eat with the family but always in his own chamber, and he made a table of his trunk. He was always achawing except some little intervalls of time in which he applied to the study of the English language.

Sunday, August 5. I went this morning into Monsieur's chamber and asked him how he did. He made answer in French but asked me in maimd English if I had made un bon voyage, what news, and many other little questions culled out of his grammar. I was shy of letting him know I understood French, being loath to speak that language as knowing my faultiness in the pronounciation. He told me that hier a soir he had de mos' excellen' *soupé* and wished I had been to eat along with him. His chamber was strangely set out: here a bason with the relicts of some soup, there a fragment of bread, here a paper of salt, there a bundle of garlick, here a spoon with some pepper in it, and upon a chair a saucer of butter. The same

5. That he may be free from base calumny.
6. Grammarians tell us why *cunnus* has masculine names/and why *mentula* (male genitals) has a feminine name.

individual bason served him to eat his soup out of and to shave in, and in the water, where a little before he had washed his hands and face, he washed likewise his cabbages. This, too, served him for a punch-bowl. He was fond of giving directions how to dress his vittles and told Nanny, the cook maid, "Ma foy, I be de good cock, Madame Nannie," said he. The maid put on an air of modest anger and said she did not understand him. "Why, here you see," says he, "my cock be good, can dress de fine viandes."

. . .

PART FOUR

The Roots of Democratic Humor

ANDROBOROS

ROBERT Hunter (d. 1734) was the royal governor of the province of New York from 1710 to 1719. Before he went to America, Hunter served in the English army under the Duke of Marlborough, and later, during the reign of William of Orange. In peacetime, he was well connected in London literary circles, having published some of his essays in the *Tatler*. He is supposed to have known Addison and Steele and upon his appointment to the colonies he was given a complimentary farewell in the *Tatler*. Hunter was originally sent to be governor of Virginia but never arrived there owing to his capture by the French.[1]

As he sailed for New York, England was in the midst of the War of the Spanish Succession (1702–1713), called "Queen Anne's War" in the colonies. In North America, this war involved the persistently unsuccessful effort to capture Canada from the French. As usual, this effort was conceived as a two-pronged attack: one from the sea and the other by land up the Hudson River Valley from New York City.

Hunter arrived as Queen Anne's royal servant in the summer of 1710, and that fall, an English expedition under Francis Nicholson (*Androboros*) managed to take Port Royal on Acadia by sea. The following year, another "two-pronged" effort was made which due to fog, poor management, and generally widespread bungling, failed, thus ending colonial efforts in Queen Anne's War. Governor Hunter played a minor role in all this shuffling about and saved his reputation by limiting himself to speeches about the need for

1. Herbert L. Osgood, *The American Colonies in the Eighteenth Century,* II (New York: Columbia University Press, 1924), 97–98.

[147]

co-operation from the New York legislature. Nicholson, whose expedition from Albany was forced to retreat southward, was more fully embroiled in the fiascos, and the news of disaster caused him to rip off his wig and shout "Roguery! Treachery!" as he jumped upon it.[2] Hunter, who had seen action in the more seriously heroic battles at Blenheim and Ramilles, probably welcomed the peace settlement which came with the Treaty of Utrecht in 1713.

Robert Hunter is considered one of the most outstandingly successful governors to rule amid the factional bitterness of New York politics.[3] Surrounded by conflicts between New England settlers on Long Island and the more western reaches of the colony, and in-fighting between the many ethnic and religious groups in the once Dutch province, Hunter was forced to do battle with the lower house of the legislature which insisted upon its own control of the colony's finances. More than any of his predecessors, Hunter succeeded, and his sense of humor contributed greatly to his political triumphs.

Hunter, ". . . an exceedingly well shaped and well proportioned man . . . ," according to a friend,[4] wrote *Androboros* because of his struggles with the obstinate assembly and his encounters with a variety of pretenders to glory and booty in the New World. He cast himself as the *Keeper* of this wild menagerie and his political ally, Lewis Morris (1671–1746) as *Solemn*. Morris helped Hunter write this satiric play, and during his own later tenure as governor of New Jersey, satirized the legislature there by asking rhetorically, "how can a man get wisdom . . . who driveth oxen and is occupied in their labor and whose talk is of bullocks?"[5] Such sentiments earned him eviction from the New York Assembly and inspired Solemn's fate in *Androboros*.

Hunter's satire of New Yorkers, Francis Nicholson, the Anglican Commissary William Vesey, and others was published in New York by William Bradford and was meant to be read by literate

2. David Hawke, *The Colonial Experience* (New York: Bobbs-Merrill, 1966), p. 333.
3. Bernard Bailyn, *The Origins of American Politics* (New York: Alfred A. Knopf, 1968), pp. 107–09.
4. Cadwallader Colden, as quoted by Osgood, *American Colonies,* II, 97.
5. As quoted by Hawke, *Colonial Experience,* p. 479.

settlers. It was well received, for according to Cadwallader Colden, "the laugh was turned upon them in all companies, and from this laughing humor the people began to be in good humour with their Governor. . . ."[6] Here lies one of the major uses of humor in eighteenth-century politics. In employing burlesque and satire, Hunter was able to deal with political divisions indirectly when directness would have led to further confrontation. The issues of royal prerogative and legislative powers were so hotly debated that laughter cooled the fires without surrender on either side.[7]

Finally, even though many of the laughs in *Androboros* were on wilderness ignorance and pretensions, the title character, "Man-Eater," was a well-placed imperial functionary, who, in the course of the action, was the butt of some wildly slapstick humiliations. This leveling of the lofty provided an acceptable means of balancing aristocratic privilege with more democratic equality. Hunter's humor clearly reflects such tensions in early eighteenth-century New York.

W.H.K.

DRAMMATIS PERSONAE[8]

Androboros [General Francis Nicholson, 1655–1728]
Keeper [Governor Robert Hunter, d. 1734]
Deputy [George Clark, 1676–1760]
Speaker [William Nicolls, 1655–1723]
Æsop [David Jamison, 1660–1739]
Doodlesack [Abraham Lakerman]
Tom of Bedlam

6. Colden in Osgood, *American Colonies*, II, 118.
7. See also: Elaine G. Breslaw, "Wit, Whimsy and Politics: The Uses of Satire by the Tuesday Club of Annapolis, 1744 to 1756," *William and Mary Quarterly,* 3d. ser., XXXII, 2 (April 1975), 304.
8. *Sic.* [Dramatis Personae]. This does not appear in the Wm. Bradford edition of 1714, available on the Readex Microprint edition of Charles Evans's *Early American Imprints.* It is presented in Walter J. Meserve and William R. Reardon, eds., *Satiric Comedies* (Bloomington: Indiana University Press, 1969), pp. 1–40.

Babilard [Samuel Bayard]
Coxcomb [Daniel Coxe, 1673–1739]
Mulligrub [Samuel Mulford, 1645–1725]
Cobus [Jacobus Van Cortland, 1658–1739]
Solemn [Lewis Morris, 1671–1746]
Door-Keeper
Fizle [Reverend William Vesey, 1674–1746]
Flip [Adolph Philipse, 1665–1750]
Messenger
Scene: Long Gallary in Moor-Fields

It is an Old Maxim, et c'est Escrit,[9]
Au trou de mon cul,[10] look there you'll sie't,
When the Head is Be—ck't the Body's Beshit,
    Which no Body dare Deny, Deny,
    Which no Body dare Deny.

But 'tis strange how Notions are chang'd of late,
For 'tis a New Maxim, but an odd one, That
Ce que pend a nos culs doit nous garnir latete,[11]
    That I flatly and boldly Deny, Deny,
    That I flatly and boldly Deny.

And it was a most Masterly stroke of Art
To give Fizle Room to Act his part;
For a Fizle restrain'd will bounce like a F—t,
    Which no Body can Deny, Deny,
    Which no Body can Deny.
But when it Escapes from Canonical Hose
And fly's in your Face, as it's odds it does,
That a Man should be hang'd for stopping his Nose,

9. More exactly: *c'est Ecrit*.
10. In my asshole.
11. In other words: *Ce qui pend à nos culs doit nous garnir la tête*. [What hangs from our asses will decorate our heads; i.e., The world is turned upsidedown.]

[150]

That I flatly and boldly Deny, Deny;
That I flatly and boldly Deny.

Long kept under Hatches, 'twill force a Vent
In the Shape of a Turd, with its Size and Scent
And perhaps in its way may beshit a Vestment,
    Which no body can Deny, Deny;
    Which no body can Deny.
But However 'tis Dignify'd or Disguis'd,
That it should be for that the higher Priz'd,
And either Don Commis'd or Canoniz'd,
    That I flatly and boldly Deny, Deny,
    That I flatly and boldly Deny.

                        B'uey Fizle.

ANDROBOROS

Act First, Scene First
KEEPER, DEPUTY *and* TOM.

DEPUTY. I Hope, Sir, it is not your intention that this same *Senate,* as they call it, should sit.

KEEPER. What harm is there in't, if it does?

DEPUTY. No great harm, only 'twill please their Frenzy; They are big with Expectation of some mighty Deliverance, towards which is to be brought about by means of *Androboros*; I think they call him so; Whether there is or ever was such a Person, I know not: but all their hopes are placed in him.

TOM. Sir, it is *Old Nick-nack,* who has Paganiz'd himself with that Name, which interpreted, signifies a *Man-Eater.* He is now very far gone indeed. He talks of nothing but Battles and Seiges, tho' he never saw one, and Conquests over Nations, and Alliances with Princes who never had a being; and this Senate is mainly

[151]

intended for his Reception. I hope you will not forbid its Meeting, if you do, I shall loose an Employment, having had the Honor to be appointed Clerk of the Senate this Morning, after the Choice of the Speaker; so I beg you'll not Rob me of that Honor, and your self of some Diversion, and I shall take care that their Session shall be harmless.

KEEPER. I wish you Joy with all my heart; But Prethee, *Tom,* What Chance or evil Fate conducted thee to this same Doleful Mansion? I am surpriz'd to find thee in such Company.

TOM. No Chance, I assure you, *Sir,* but free Choice. I found in my reading, That Man was composed of three parts, *Body, Soul* and *Spirit,* and that the two first were entirely ingross'd by two Societys, so I resolv'd to Exercise my poor Talent upon the Infirmitys of the last, not with any hopes or intention to Cure them, but as others do, meerly to raise my self a Maintenance out of them, here under your Honors happy Auspeces. But, Lo, here they come. Retire to a Corner. If I am seen in your Company, my Project is spoyl'd.

Act First, Scene Second
Enter DOODLESACK, BABILARD, SOLEMN, ÆSOP, &C.

SPEAKER. Gentlemen, The Honor you have done me, how little soever I may deserve it, lays me under an Obligation to Exert my self to the utmost for the interest of this House. I humbly propose, That in the first place we concert and agree upon some necessary Rules for preventing Confusion.

DEPUTY. [*aside*]—Well spoke, Mr. Speaker, Tho' 'tis something strange that he who has ever affirm'd, That Laws and Liberty were things Incompatible, should now propose to proceed by Rules.

MULLIGRUB. I desire to be heard before you proceed to Rules, or any thing else; I have a Speech ready.

DOODLESACK. Laet onse hearken to Mr. Speaker, and begin with some Rules.

MULLIG. I'll have my Speech first.

[152]

COXCOMB. D—n your Speech, Let's proceed to Rules.

BABILARD. If Rules be necessary to the Speech, let us have the Speech first, but if the Speech be necessary to the Rules, let us have the Rules.

COX. I'm for neither Speech nor Rules, let us fall upon buss'ness.

SPEAKER. Gentlemen, The Question is not, as I take it, which you'll be pleas'd to have, but which shall have the Preference; for you may have both in their Turns.

ALL. [*Confusedly.*] Speech, Rules; Rules, Speech, &c.

MULLIGRUB. My Speech has carry'd it. Hum, Ha, Ough, Ough, Ough, Ough, Ough, &c.

COX. Rot ye, it was not your Cough that Carry'd it; Let off your Speech.

ÆSOP. Mr. Speaker, I do not find that this matter is, as yet, determin'd to the full satisfaction of this House, for which Cause I beg leave to offer an Expedient, which will end the Debate, that is, That we may have both at a time; whilst Mr. *Mulligrub* is Exonerating himself, we may imploy our selves in adjusting and forming the necessary Rules.

ALL. Agreed.

SPEAKER. Mr. *Mulligrub,* You may proceed.

MULL. Gentlemen, The ill Measures that have been taken, and the Foundation that hath been laid within this Tenement, to make the Tenents thereof, Tenants therein, is the Cause which causeth me to make this Speech. Our Grievances being innumerable, I shall Enumerate them. The first I shall mention, is this, That tho' the Tenement be large, the Mansions many, and the Inhabitants Numerous, There is but One Kitchin, and one Cellar, by which means we are kept from Eating and drinking What we please, When we please, and as Much as we please, which is our Birth-Right Priviledge by the Laws of God and Nature, settled upon us by Act of Parliament; for which cause I humbly [ask the] House Whether it may not be more Convenient that each Mansion have its proper Kitchin and Cellar under the special Direction of the respective Tenants?

[153]

To clear up the Necessity of this Method, I'll tell you what happ'ned to me t'other day; One of the Servants of this House, who brought me a Mess of Water Gruel, being my special Friend, and knowing how eagerly my Stomach stood towards what was forbidden me by the Physicians, conveys a Hand of Pork into the Porrige, but being discover'd he was punisht, tho' he offer'd to take his Corporal Oath, That the Hand of Pork was a bunch of Radishes. But of all others, we of the East End of the Tenement suffer most, for by reason of our distance from the Kitchin, our Porrige is cold before it comes to our Hands. To Remedy this, we fell upon a private Intercourse with the Bethlemites on the other side of *Moor-fields,* [12] who by virtue of their Charter run at large, by which we broke the Laws pretty Comfortably for a season; but these same subtle Fellows of the Kitchin found it out, and put a stop to't, to the Great Prejudice of the Freedom of the Subject, and the direct Discouragement of our indirect Commerce. I Remember we once Address'd our Superiors, That we might have a Servant of our own, independent of this Plaguey *Keeper*; They were Graciously pleas'd to allow us such a one, with this Restriction only, That the Servant aforesaid might have the Custody of our Straw and Water, but by no means of our Meat and Drink; notwithstanding this, the Keeper will not permit him to take the care and Custody of our Victuals and Drink. What! does he think us *Non Corpus Mentlus,* that we do not know the meaning of plain words! But *I* shall Conclude at this time, with this Exhortation, That since it appears plainly, that we of this Tenement, who are Tenants thereof, are in danger of Being, by the Foundations laid, made Tenants therein, let us not lie Crying thereat, but be Valiant Therefore, and Vindicate our Rights Therefrom, Our Birth-Right Parliamentary Rights, settled upon us by the Ten Commandments.

SPEAKER. Gentlemen, Mr. *Mulligrub* has given you time to Concert the Rules of the House, would you have them read by the Clerk, in the Order they have been given to him by the several Members?

12. In other words, the inhabitants of the insane asylum Bethlehem Hospital, located in a partially-filled swamp north of London, called Moorfields (now Finsbury).

ALL. Ay, Ay.

TOM. [*Reads*] Mr. *Speaker* Proposes, That to prevent Confusion, not above Three or Four at most be permitted to speak at Once, except in a Grand committee, where there is no occasion of Hearers.

Mr. *Coxcomb* humbly proposes, That no Body be allow'd to speak but himself, because for want of the Attentive Faculty, he is like to have no share in the Hearing, and so ought to have Compensation in Speaking.

Doodlesack has given his in a Forreign Tongue, which when interpreted stands thus, That He having but a small share of Elocution, but a very lively and strong imagination, may have leave, as occasion shall offer, to Express his Thoughts by Staring, Grinning and Grimacing, of which he has so Exquisite a Talent, that those who cannot be said to understand any thing else, perfectly understand him in that Method of Utterance.

Babilardus Represents, That he is quite Dum-founded by the late fall of Stocks, so in Order to the opening his Mouth, he proposes a Law for raising Int'rest to *Twelve per Cent*.

AEsop has given his Rule in Rhime, as follows,

> The Rule that I would advise,
> Is to Be quiet, and eat your Bread,
> If 'tis good; To be Merry and Wise.
> 'Tis the Dev'l to be Sullen and Mad.

COXCOMB. Damn all Rules, Let us proceed to buss'ness.

COBUS. Laet onze erst come to some Revoluties.

COXCOM. Resolutions! Ay, begin with that, I like that Motion well enough; it is the shortest way.

SPEAKER. Let one at a time Propose, and the rest Agree or Dissent, as they think fit.

COXCOM. Resolv'd That neither this House, or they whom we Represent are bound by any Laws, Rules or Customs, any Law, Rule or Custom to the Contrary Notwithstanding.

[155]

ALL. Agreed.

MULLIGR. That this House disclaims all Powers, Preheminencies or Authoritys, except it's own.

ALL. Agreed.

BABILARD. That this House has an Inherent and Undoubted Right to the Undoubted Property of those we Represent.

COXCOMB. That this House is the only Undoubted Supreme Inferior and Infimus Court of this Tenement, and that all others are a Nusance.

ALL. Agreed.

SOLEMN. Mr. Speaker, being Resolv'd to enter my Dissent to these several Resolves, I shall first give my Reasons for so doing. I believe it is needless to put you in mind of our Origine, from whence we sprang, and how we came hither. It is well known that we were of that Number of Publick Spirited Persons, distinguish't from our Neighbours by an inward Light or Faculty, call it what you Please. The *Romans* call it *AEstrum,* The *French, Verve,* our Northern Nation has indeed given it a Courser Name, which gave us a strong Disposition toward Reformations, Remonstrations, Resolutions, and other Acts of Zeal; in the eager pursuit of which we were apt to throw our selves, sometimes our Neighbours, into the Fire or Water. The Wisdom of the Times thought fit to Erect this Tenement for our Intertainment, where the Exercize of the Faculty aforesaid might be less Dangerous or hurtful to our selves, or others. Here we are Maintain'd at their Charge with Food and Rayment suitable to our Condition, and the Fabrick kept in Repair at the no small Annual Expences of our Land-Lords. And what Returns do we make? Have not many of us from our private Cells thrown our Filth and Ordure in their Faces? And now in a Collective Body we are about to throw more filthy Resolves at them.

ALL. To the Barr, to the Barr.

ALL. No, With-draw, With-draw.

SOLEMN. I desire to be heard.

ALL. With-draw.

SPEAKER. *Sir,* It is the pleasure of this House that you Withdraw, in order to your being heard. [*Exit* SOLEMN]

[156]

Gentlemen, your [*sic*] have heard this mans Insolence. What shall be done with him?

COXCOMB. Hang'd, Drawn and Quarter'd.

ÆSOP. Ay, but what is his Crime?

COXCOM. For affronting the Majesty of this House.

ÆSOP. In what? What has he done or said?

COBUS. Dat weet ick niet, but I agree with Coxcombs Propositie.

SPEAKER. I am for Inflicting no Punishment but what is in our Power, that is, to Expell him the House.

ALL. Expell, Expell.

ÆSOP. Hold a little. I suppose you intend to punish him, and not your selves; I'll tell you a Story.

ALL. Expell, Expell, &c.

ÆSOP. I beg your Patience, 'tis but a short one; it is a Tale of a Pack of Hounds of my Acquaintance,

> *Fowler,* the stanchest Hound o'th' breed,
> Had got th' ill Will of all the rest;
> Not for his Tongue, his Nose or Speed,
> Tho' these were all by far the best;
> Malice and Envy know no bounds
> And Currs have ever bark'd at Hounds.
> But that which most provok'd their Spite
> Was this, that when they run a Foil
> Or Counter, *Fowler* led them right,
> Which cost him many a bitter broil,
> Snubbing the Rash and Rioters,
> And lugging laizy Ones by th' Ears.
>
> So at a General Council held
> For Grievances, ow what you will,
> Poor trusty *Fowler* was Expell'd,
> That free-born Dogs might range their fill.
> And so they did; but mark what came on't,
> Hence-forth they made but sorry Game on't.

[157]

The giddy Pack, their Guide b'ing gone,
Run Riot, and the Hunts-Man swore,
Scrap't some, and some he whipt; but one
He hang'd, a Noisy babling Curr.

In short, the Pack was spoyl'd; Pray then,
Shall *Fowler* be Expell'd agen?

COXCOMB. A Pox on your Tale, let us proceed to the Vote.
SPEAKER. What is then your pleasure with relation to the
Member who is to be Expell'd?
ALL. Expell'd, Expell'd.
SPEAKER. Call him to the Bar.

[*Enter* SOLEMN.]

Sir, For *Reasons* best known to our selves, you are Expell'd.
SOLEMN. *Sir,* You do me too much honour. [*Exit.*]

[*Enter* MESSENGER.]

MESSENGER. Mr. *Speaker,* The Lord *Androboros* with Two
Men in Black desires Admittance.
SPEAKER. Is it your pleasure he be admitted?
OMNES. Ay, Ay.
SPEAKER. Let the Clerk go to him with the Compliments of the
House, and Conduct him in [TOM *a going*]
KEEPER. St. St. St. *Tom,* a Word with you. Pray who are these
same men in Black, who accompany the General?
TOM. Two other special Friends of yours, *viz. Fizle* and *Flip;*
The first was heretofore a *Muggletonian*[13] of the other side of
Moor-fields, but having no Butter to his Bread there, he Chang'd

13. Follower of Lodowick Muggleton (1609–1698), a Puritan sectarian imprisoned for
blasphemy. His followers believed him a prophet.

[158]

their *Service* for that of this House; He sometime fancy'd himself to be the Pope, but his Brother not relishing that as Derogatory to his Pretensions, he is now Contented to be Patriarch of the Western Empire, of which *Androboros* is to be Sultan; The other, for a wonderful Energy in the two most Unruly Members of the Body, has been follow'd of late by the Women and Boys, but a late sinistrous Accident has Crack't his Voice, and—that now he is but little regarded. But I must be gone. [*Ex.* TOM]

KEEPER. The Rogue is a good Painter.

DEPUTY. He draws from the Life, I assure you.

Act First, Scene Third
Enter ANDROBOROS *and* TOM, FLIP *and* FIZLE.

ANDROB. Most Venerable Gentlemen, Upon my Rounds of Inspection, Prospection and Retrospection, I have understood with Pleasure, that you have sequester'd from your House that wandring Plague, that Kibes in the Heels,[14] and Piles in the posteriors of Mankind.

ÆSOP. Pardon me, Sir, your Name has not been mention'd here, that I know of.

ANDROB. I mean *Solemn,* which Act I approve and Commend. It is with no less satisfaction that I now acquaint you, That upon the Earnest Application and most humble Suit of the High and Po tent *TOWROWMOWYOUGHTOUGH,* Emperor of many Nations, and my good Allies, the Kings of *AGNISAG-KIMAGHSWOUGHSAYK, SAVANAGHTIPHIUGH,* and *BOWWOUGEWOUFFE,* I have undertaken an Expedition against the *Mulo Machians,* your Inveterate Foes. Your Concurrence to enable me to carry it on with Success, is what I demand and expect; and for your Incouragement, I do swear by this sacred Image, not to pare these Nails, wash this blew Visage, or put off the speckled *Shirt,* Until I have made that Haughly Monarch Confess himself, in all his Projects for Universal Dominion, my Inferior, and My Delamya, fairer then the fairest Princess of his Blood or

14. Chilblains in the heels.

[159]

Empire. So leaving this weighty Affair to your wise Counsels, We bid you heartily Farewell. [*Exit Strutting*]

SPEAKER. You have heard what this Man has propos'd. What do you Resolve?

COXCOM. Let us Resolve to Support, Maintain and Defend the undoubted Title of the Great *Androboros* to the Powers and Au-thoritys he has Graciously Assum'd over this and all other the like Tenements, against all Wardens, Directors, Keepers, and their Abettors.

ALL. Agreed.

DOODLESACK. Laet onze Dissolve, That a Summ not Exceed-ing Negen Skillingen and Elleve Pence be rais'd for the Expeditie.

ALL. Agreed.

SPEAKER. Ay, and 'tis more than 'tis worth.

BABILARD. Let us Resolve, That He has behav'd Himself on the said Expedition with Courage, Conduct and Prudence.

SPEAKER. What! before 'tis over!

ÆSOP. By all means, lest when it is over you should have less reason for this Resolve. But if after all, we must go to War, I would be glad to be better satisfy'd with the Choice of a Leader; For as to this Man's Prowess, we have nothing but his own Word for't.

COXCOMB. The Choice is a good Choice, and he that doubts it, is a Son— — — So for that, amongst other weighty Reasons, I second Mr. *Babilards* Motion.

DOODLESACK. Ick Ock, because it may cast some Reflectie upon our Keeper. . . .

Act First, Scene Fourth.
Enter KEEPER *and* DEPUTY

KEEPER. To your Kennels, ye Hounds.—[*Exit* OMNES]

DEPUTY. Now, *Sir,* I hope you are satisfied, and for the future you'll keep 'em to their Cells.

KEEPER. No, let them enjoy their former Liberty, perhaps they'll stand Corrected.

DEPUTY. I much doubt it; but I shall Obey.

[160]

KEEPER. Now, Mr. *Tom*. If I may be so bold, Favour me with a sight of the Minutes of your House.

TOM. With all my heart, here they are.

KEEPER. What's here! A *Castle,* a *Wind-Mill,* and *Shephard* with a *Ram* at his back?

TOM. Ay, *Sir*, a sort of Ægyptian short Hand, containing the substance of their Resolves. The *Castle Renvers'd* and in the Air, denotes the independency of our House; The *Wind-Mill* without Sails, an Expedition without Means or Leader; and the *Ram* butting the *Shephard on the Breech,* or in other words, dismissing him from having any further Authority over him.—

KEEPER. That wants no Explanation. You'll Watch them, *Tom*, and serve them in the same Capacity, if they meet again.

TOM. To the best of my Skill.

KEEPER. Lets to Dinner. [*Exeunt*]

Finis Actus Primi

Act Second, Scene First.
Enter BABILARD, FIZLE, FLIP, COXCOMB

BABILARD. You see what our wise Resolves have brought upon us, we shall never do this buss'ness in this way, Muzled as we are; I wish my Advice had been follow'd.

FIZLE. Pray what was that?

BABILARD. I was for proceeding in the way of secret Representations and Remonstrances against him, which My Lord Oinobaros, his declar'd Enemy, might have long e'er this improv'd to his Ruin.

FIZLE. That was my own Method, but that which discourages me is, that at Parting my Lord assur'd me, That he would return in six Moneths, and Confirm me in my Patriarchat; instead of that, he has himself taken up with the Wardenship of a Sprunging-house.[15]

COXCOMB. No, that Method will never do. Have not I, and my Friends transmitted to Mr. *Wry Rump* a Ream of Complaints, as

15. House of prostitution.

[161]

big as the Bunch on his back, which were Referr'd to the Consideration of the Casually sitting Members of the little House, and he was
dismiss'd with a Kick o'th' Breech. We must Accuse him of
something more Flagrant; Triffles won't do.

FIZLE. Why, Then I have another Device for you. You see he
can Dissolve our Senate with a Crack of his Whip, so there is
nothing to be done that way. Let us incorporate our selves into a
Consistory; That I believe He dare not touch, without being
Reputed an Enemy to the Consistory; and if he does, we may hunt
him down full Cry at present.

FLIP. That I shold like well enough, but I'm afraid the Cunning
Rogue won't meddle with us, as such.

FIZLE. We'll say, and swear, That he did, and that's all one. I
have a Plot in my head, which I hope will do the buss'ness; in the
mean time, go you and acquaint the Rest, that they meet us here in
full Consistory Immediately. [*Exit* BABILARD, *and* COXCOM]

FLIP. Pray, Brother, Instruct me in your Contrivance, I may
help you out with my Advice.

FIZLE. It is briefly this. This same Rogue was ever an Enemy to
the short Coats and Scanty Skirts of the Laity, and Consequently to
the long Robes and Pudding Sleeves of the others; I'll instantly
have my long Coat Beskirted and Besh— — —, and give out, That
it is He, or some of his People, who has don't. If any should be so
Heterodox as to doubt the truth o'nt, I have some ready to swear to
the Size and Color of the T———.

FLIP. I like this well; about it streight, I'll attend them here,
Open the Consistory in your Names, and Prepare 'em for what is to
ensue. [*Exit* FIZLE]

FLIP. This same Fizle is a Notable Fellow for the head of a
Consistory, if he had but a Competent Doze of Brains; but These
are so shallow that a Louse may suck 'em up without surfeiting,
which renders that noble Portion of *Malice,* with which he is
Liberally endow'd of little use to the Publick.

Act Second, Scene Second

Enter MULLIGRUB, DOODLESACK, BABILARD, COXCOMB,
TOM, ÆSOP &C.

[162]

FLIP. In the Absence of My Brother *Fizle* whose occasions have call'd him away for a little time, I am to acquaint you, That he has of his own free Will, meer Motion and by virtue of the Plentitude of his Patriarchal Authority, chosen and elected you for his Consistory-men and Counsellors in all Cases and Causes Visable and Invisable.

COXCOM. We are highly honor'd by his Choice, and Promise an Implicit Obedience to his pleasure.   [*Enter* FIZLE]

FIZLE. O Horror! O Abomination! was ever the like seen, heard or read of!

FLIP. What's the Matter?

FIZLE. As I went to Robe my self for the more decent Attendance on this Consistory I found my Robes in this Pickle! That Vestment, so Reverenc'd by the Antient and Modern World, beskirted and Bedaub'd with what I must not name!

ÆSOP. Who has done this?

FIZLE. Who has done it! Who but the known Enemies to Consistorys and Long Skirts?

ÆSOP. But methinks your Discretion should have directed you to our Keeper with this Complaint.

FIZLE. Our Keeper! One of my Brethren told him of it but now, and he coldly Reply'd, If Mr. *Fizle* from the Redundancy of his Zeal has beshit himself, the Abundance of his Wisdom, methinks, should prevail with him to keep the Secret, and make himself Clean.

MULLIGR. A plain Proof the Keeper is the Man.

COXCOMB. Ay, Ay, There Needs No Other Proof; it must be the Keeper.

FIZLE. I own, I thought so from the beginning; but what course shall we steer for Redress?

FLIP. If I may be thought worthy to advise in a matter of this Moment, we shall immediately Address My Lord Oinobaros on this head, he being a Devotee to Long Robes of both Gendres, must highly Resent this Affront, and with the Assistance of *Androboros,* no less an Enemy to the Keeper, may Manage it to his Ruin and our Satisfaction.

[163]

BABIL. Let Mr. *Fizle* draw up an Address, and we'll all sign it.

FIZLE. Gentlemen, If such is your pleasure, I'll retire with the Clerk, prepare one, and submit it to your Approbation.

ALL. Pray go about it. [*Exit* FIZLE *and* TOM]

ÆSOP. I Resent this Affront to the Long Robe as much as any Man, but methinks you proceed too hastily, and upon too slender Grounds against your Keeper. We all know the Malice of Mr. *Fizle's* heart, and that it has Increas'd in proportion to the Keepers good Nature. Had he been oftner Check'd, he had been less Troublesome to himself and us. Let us not provoke our Keeper; for my part, I think he is a good one.

COXCOM. What! is he not an Enemy to the Consistory?

ÆSOP. No, he is an Enemy to their Folly . . .

Act Second, Scene Third
Enter FIZLE *and* TOM

FIZLE. Gentlemen, I have finish'd the Address. Is it your pleasure that the Clerk read it?

ALL. Ay, Ay.

TOM. [*Reads*] To the most Potent Lord Oinobaros, Count of *Kynommatia,* Baron of *Elaphokardia,* The General Consistory of *New Bed—l—m* most Humbly Represent, That we your Excellencies ever *Besorted Subjects.*

FIZLE. Devoted Subjects.

TOM. Under a deep sense of the manifold *Bastings* we Enjoy'd.

FIZLE. *Blessings,* you Ouph you.

TOM. Blessings we Enjoy'd under your *Wild Administration.*

FIZLE. Mild Administration.

TOM. Mild Administration, find our selves at this time under a *Nonsensical Inclination.*

FIZLE. What's that? Let me see't, *Non-sensical Inclination!* It can't be so; It is *Indispensible Obligation.*

TOM. Ay, it should be so.

FIZLE. Write it down so then.

TOM. 'Tis done. Finding our selves under an *Incomprehensible Obstination.*

[164]

FLIP. 'Owns! That's worse than t'other.

TOM. Cry Mercy, That is a blunder, *Indispensible Obligation* to have Recourse to your Excellencies known *Condemnable Opposition* to our Consistory, and all Things Sacred.

FIZLE. I think the Dev'l is in the Fellow. It is *Commendable Disposition*.

TOM. You use so many Long Words, that a Clerk who is not a Scholar may easily mistake one for another. Towards our Consistory, and all things Sacred, Take Leave humble to Represent, That on the *Ev'ning which succeeded the following Day.*

FIZLE. Thou Eternal Dunce! *The Ev'ning which preceded All-hallowday.*

TOM. Which preceded *All-hallowday* some open or secret Enemies to this Consistory broke into our *Cupboard.*

FIZLE. Ward-Robe.

TOM. Wardrobe, taking from thence some Lumber appertaining to the *Chief of our Rogues,* I mean, some Robes appertaining to the Chief of our Number, which they Inhumanely Tore to pieces and Bedaub'd with *Odour.*

MULLIGRUB. Hold! I make Exception to that, for there are sweet Odors as well as sower.

FLIP. 'Slid; 'tis *Ordure,* (and not *Odour*) which is but another Name for a T—d.

MULLIGR. Write it down so then, for a T——— is a T——— all the world over.

ÆSOP. And the more you stir it, the more 'twill stink. But go on.

TOM. Now tho' we *cannot Possibly Prove,* yet we *Affirm Positively,* That it is our Keeper.

ÆSOP. How's that?

FIZLE. He reads wrong; it is, *Tho' we cannot Positively Prove yet we Affirm,* That *possibly it may be our Keeper.* Go on.

TOM. Our Keeper, or some of his People, who is guilty of this *Facetious Fact.*

FIZLE. Flagitious Fact.

TOM. Flagitious Fact. We further beg leave to Represent, That this Morning in a Collective Body, by a great *Brutality of Noises.*

[165]

FIZLE. Plurality of Voices.

TOM. We had declar'd him a *Raskal,* but he had the Impudence to send us packing to our Cells . . . Wherefore it is our humble and earnest Supplication, That we may be once more put under your *Wild Distraction.*

FIZLE. Mild Direction.

TOM. Or that of the *Excrement Androborus.*

FIZLE. Excellent *Androborus* . . . Gentlemen, do you approve of this Draught?

ÆSOP. I like it as the Clerk read it.

MULLIGRUB. I approve of all, except the *Ordure;* I'll have it a T———:

COXCOM. You'll have it a T———, a T——— in your Teeth; it shall stand as it is *Ordure.*

. . .

DOOR-KEEPER. Here's a Courier from *Androboros,* just return'd from the Expedition, who desires Admittance.

ÆSOP. It is the most Expeditious Expedition I ever heard of; let us adjourn the Address, and receive the General's Message.

FIZZLE. Let him come in. [*Enter* MESSENGER]

MESSENGER. The Renown'd *Androboros* with a tender of his hearty Zeal and Affection sends this to the *Consistory,* the Senate being Discontinued. [*delivers a Letter*].

FIZLE. [*Reads*] Right Frightful and Formidable, We Greet you Well, And by this Acquaint you, That for many Weighty Considerations Us thereunto moving, We have thought fit to adjourn the Intended Expedition to a more proper season, because we have, upon due and Mature Examination been fully convinc'd, that the *Mulomachians,* our Reputed Enemies, are in very deed our good and faithful Friends and Allies, who, to remove all Doubts and Scruples, have freely offer'd to Consolidate Consistories with us, as also to divide with us the Commerce of the World, generously resigning and yielding to us that of the two Poles, reserving to themselves only what may lie between e'm. They have likewise Condescended that we shall keep some Forts and Holds, which by

[166]

the Fortune of the War they could not take from us, and have promis'd and engag'd to Raze and Demolish some Places in their Possession to our prejudice, so soon as more Convenient are built in their room and place. You are further to understand, to your Great satisfaction, that this is a Treaty Litteral and Spiritual, so that having two Handles it may be Executed with the greater Facility, or if need be, the One may Execute the other, and so it may Execute it self. Now these Concessions (tho' it be well known that I hate Boasting) having been obtain'd, in a great measure, by the Terror of my Name and Arms, I expect your Thanks. And so we bid you heartily *Farewell*.

Androboros.

ÆSOP. Buzzzzz, Hummmm, Buzzzzz—

FIZLE. What Return shall we give to this Civil and Obliging Message?

ÆSOP. Return him his Letter.

COXCOMB. No, let us vote him Thanks, a Statue and a Triumph! [*Enter* KEEPER.]

KEEPER. Be not surpriz'd, I have heard what you are about, and Cordially joyn with you in what you propose, in honour of the Valiant *Androboros,* Having received instructions from my Superiors to use that mighty Man according to his Deserts.

ÆSOP. What! Is our Keeper Mad, too?

KEEPER. In the Mean time, all Retire to your respective Apartments, until due Dissposition be made for his Reception. [*Exit manent* FIZLE *and* ÆSOP]

Act Second, Scene Fourth

FIZLE. What Man! I'th Dumps, because our Keeper let fall a word or two about Orders to use a certain great Man according to his deserts!

ÆSOP. I hope he has receiv'd the same Orders relating to you.

FIZLE. There is more in this than you Imagine; I ever believ'd, that it would come to this at last.

[167]

ÆSOP. Why? What's the matter?

FIZLE. The Keeper undoubtedly has receiv'd Orders to resign to *Androboros*.

ÆSOP. What then?

FIZLE. What then! I'll tell you what then; Then My Brethren and I shall have our due, and you with yours be proud to lick the Dust off our Feet. . . .

Act Third, Scene First
Enter KEEPER, DEPUTY, TOM *and* SERVANT

DEPUTY. With all due Submission, Sir, give me leave to ask you what you mean by the splendid Reception you have promis'd to give to that Old Man?

KEEPER. Very little besides Diversion. My Superiors, as I am inform'd, have Cloath'd him with Sham-Powers meerly to get rid of his Noise and Trouble; and since these must fall to my share, I'll humour him to keep him quiet.

DEPUTY. That is not to be hop'd for whilst he lives.

TOM. Persuade him that he is dead then.

KEEPER and DEPUTY. Ha, Ha, Ha.

TOM. It is far from Impossible, however Extravagant you may think the Overture. If you'll be rul'd by me, I'll answer for the Success of what I propose, under any Penalties you please. I'm sure he has had the Art to Dream himself into Notions every whit as Absurd. His Imagination is very ductile when 'tis heated, and by a Long Practice upon't, he has made it as susceptible of Impressions from Without, as it has been of these from Within. Do you but when he appears, behave your selves as if he were Invisible, and take no maner of Notice of what he shall say or do, and I'll answer for the rest. Here he comes, mind him not. [*Enter* ANDROBOROS]

TOM. I was not present, *Sir,* when he Expir'd, but arriv'd a few Minutes after.

KEEPER. So suddenly too! I wish he may not have had foul play.

ANDROB. Your Servant, Gentlemen, I hope I do not Interrupt you; pray, who is it you speak of?

[168]

TOM. No, Sir, he dy'd of an uncommon Disease, The Physitians call it, a *Tympany in the Imagination,* occasion'd by a collection of much Indigested Matter there, which for the want of due Excretion, made a breach in the Pericrane, at which that great Soul took its flight.

KEEPER. Had he made his Will?

ANDROBOROS. Pray, Gentlemen, who is it that's Dead?

TOM. I have not heard of any.

ANDROB. Cry mercy, I thought—

TOM. Only about the time he Expir'd, he Cry'd, I leave This World, this Worthless World to My Delamya, O Delamya!

ANDROB. You Impudent Dog you, dare but to Profane that sacred Name with thy base breath, and I'll crush thee to Nothing.

TOM. Hark, did you not hear an odd Noise?

DEPUTY. Something like the Humming of a Bee.

TOM. Me thinks it sounded rather like the Breath of the Bung of an Empty Barrel.

ANDROB. You Sawcy Knave, Take that. [*Strikes him a Box o'th' Ear*]

TOM. It was nothing but a Flea in my Ear. [*Scratching his Ear*] And so, (as I was saying,) with that Name in his Mouth he Expir'd.

ANDROB. Gentlemen, I am not to be made a May-Game, your betters shall be acquainted with your Conduct. [*Exit*]

KEEPER. Run, *Tom,* and allay or baulk his Fury. [Exit TOM] What d'ye think of Tom's project, is it Not an Odd One?

DEPUTY. I hardly believe He'll succeed, but if he does, what then!

KEEPER. Then We shall live at ease, he'll dream no more, when he thinks that he's dead. It is amazing that this Mans Visions, like Yawning, should be catching. The Inhabitants of this Tenement are not the only Dupes of his *Quixotism.*

DEPUTY. That Indeed is matter of Wonder; and if the Countenance given to Folly be not all Grimace, The World is as Mad as he. [*Enter* TOM.]

TOM. I have Instructed the Porter, and the other Servants, and have proclaim'd to all, the General remains *Incognito,* until he

[169]

makes his Publick Entry, and that no notice is to be taken of him, more then if he were Absent, under the Pain of his highest Displeasure.

KEEPER. So far all goes well. But you must Intrust SOLEMN and ÆSOP with your Plot.

TOM. I have already. The first is to be my Conjurer.

KEEPER. Conjurer!

TOM. Yes, my Conjurer; To him alone, and that too but some times, he shall be visible, to all besides, a shadow, an Empty Name. Here they come. [*Enter* SOLEMN *and* ÆSOP]

KEEPER. Gentlemen, you have your Q.

SOLEMN. Do you but keep your Countenance, leave the rest to us. [*Chairs and a Table; they sit down. Enter* ANDROBOROS]

ANDROB. Sure all the World is Mad, or have a mind to make me so; I try'd to get out, but the Porter lean't his Staff against my Nose, and belch't full in my Chops; a Culverine[16] could not have done more suddain Execution than that Erruption of Barm and Tobacco Smoak.

SOLEMN. When is he to be Interr'd?

TOM. This Ev'ning, but is to lie in State here till then.

ANDROBOROS. I made a Shift to recover my self, and attempted the back passage; but in the Door of the Kitchin I was saluted with a Pale of foul Water, which had like to have been succeeded by a Shovel of burning Coals, but that I made a speedy Retreat. Something's the matter, what e'er it is; I'll listen here and find it out.

KEEPER. But why so suddainly? 'Tis strange so Great a Man should be bury'd with so little Ceremony.

ANDROB. Bury'd, said he!

TOM. It is done by the advice of Physitians, who have declar'd that his Disease was such as makes a man stink vilely after he is dead.

KEEPER. The fair *Delamya*! how does she bear the loss?

TOM. She's Inconsolable, ready to burst her sides.

KEEPER. How! *Tom*? Yes, Sir, Excess of Joy makes some

16. Handgun; later, a cannon.

[170]

People Weep; Excess of Grief makes her Laugh Inordinately, and Cry out Incessantly, *Are these our promised Joys, O Androboros! One Grave shall hold us.* And then she laughs again.

ANDROB. *Androboros,* it seems then I'm dead; 'tis odd that I should not know it. I'll try that. [*Takes a Chair*]

KEEPER. Poor Lady, she lov'd him well, I doubt she'll be as good as her Word.

ÆSOP. Who set this Empty Chair by me?

SOLEMN. Save me, ye Kinder Powers, and guard my Senses!

KEEPER. What's the matter, Man? What d'ye see?

TOM. It is but a Raving fit, the Effect of deep study; he is often taken so.

SOLEMN. No, my sense is temperate as yours. Look there, There [*Points.*]

ÆSOP. There is a Chair, What then? [*Shoveing it with his foot*]

SOLEMN. Have ye no Eyes? Can't you see?

KEEPER. For my part I see nothing but what I use to see.

SOLEMN. Why there, in that Chair sits the Venerable Form of the deceas'd *Androboros,* in nothing differing from that Awful Figure he once made, but that you regard it not.

KEEPER. Sure he Raves.

ÆSOP. That Chair. Why there's nothing in that Chair. There it lies. [*Strikes down* ANDROBOROS, *Chair and all*]

SOLEMN. O! Offer it no Violence.

ANDROB. You Old Dog, I'll be Reveng'd. [*Goes off*]

SOLEMN. See how it Stalks off! With what Majestick Air, and how Stern a Brow! It Resents the Indignity offer'd. Ha, Ha, Ha.

ALL. Ha, Ha, Ha, Ha.

TOM. Now we have him; it begins to work, if I do not mistake his Looks.

DEPUTY. I had much ado to contain my self.

KEEPER. What's next to be done?

TOM. Trust that to me; but be sure not to mind him, ev'n tho' he should be Outragious. To *Solemn* only he must be visible for some time. Have you got your Conjuring Tackle ready?

SOLEMN. I have, That will serve the turn. O here he comes

[171]

again in very pensive Mood and doleful Dumps. All walk off, as if you saw him not; I'll remain alone. [*Exeunt* KEEPER, DEPUTY, TOM *and* ÆSOP, *passing by* ANDROBOROS *without taking Notice of him*]

Act Third, Scene Second
SOLEMN *at the Table with Books and Implements. Enter* AN-DROBOROS.

ANDROB. 'Tis Strange, Wondrous strange, I should take the whole to be a Trick, were it not that my best, my firmest Friends, who never could be Induc'd to practice upon me in this gross manner, behave themselves to my Face as if they saw me not. Whilst I sate at the Table, That only Raskal, *Solemn* saw me, and started and star'd as if he had seen a Ghost; The Rest saw nothing. They were talking of my Disease, Death, Burial and latter Will, as of things certain, and of publick knowledge. I think I'm pretty sure that I am Alive, tho' it seems, I am singular in that belief. I See, I Feel, I Hear as I us'd to do, ev'n now I hear my own Voice as plain as can be; I have Thought and Reflection as usual. But, Alas! departed Spirits if they think at all, must think that they do think, that is, that they are not dead,—It may be so—Ev'n that very Knave who but now could see me, sits musing by himself as if I were not here. I Remember it was the Common Opinion that a Ghost that walks, could be seen but by One of a Company. But why should he be blind now? [*Walks nearer*]

SOLEMN. It must Portend some suddain Change i 'th' State; For Ghosts of Note never walk but upon these solemn Errands.

ANDROB. He does not see me yet; I remember I was on th' other side when he saw me last. [*Goes to the other side*]

SOLEMN. If the poor Spirit is permitted once more to haunt these Walls, I'll question it, if my Courage fail me not; he may, perhaps, have something of Moment in Commission.

ANDROB. If you can't see me, can't you hear me, you old Dev'l you? [*Bawling*] . . . [*Exit*]

ANDROB. Unsear your Ears, ye Old Buzzard, I can speak, but

[172]

you, it seems, can't hear. He's gone, a Pestilence go with him. . . . I am Dead, as sure as I'm Alive; Dead, Dead as a Herring, and something worse too; for I am Condemn'd to Converse with no Body, but Old *Solemn,* who ever was a Hell upon Earth to me. . . . [*Enter* TOM *with a Broom Sweeping the Galley*]

TOM. What a Clutter is here about the Earthing an Old Stinking Corps; Would he had Lain in State in some other place; but rest his Soul, such was his Will. [*Sings*]

> *Whenas* Old Nick-Nack *Rul'd this Land,*
> *A Doughty Blade he wore.*
> *Four Dozen dragons Hides he Tann'd,*
> *Of Gyants eke Four Score.*

ANDROB. I wonder if the Ghosts of other Men hear all the Vile Things that are said and Sung of them after their Death? [TOM *sweeps the Dust on him*]

TOM. *But now he's Dead, and laid in Clay.* —This Dust most Abominably Salt, I must qualify't a little. [*Drinks, and spurts it upon him*] What a Plaguy Earthy Taste this same small Beer has got, all of a suddain. [*Sings*]

But now he's Dead and laid in Clay, —

ANDROB. That's a Lye, for I a'n't Bury'd yet, by his own Confession.

TOM.

> *Alack, and Wo therefore,*
> *The Gyants they may go to play,*
> *The Dragons sleep and snore.*

What a Carrion stink there is; the more I sweep the more it stinks. . . . I'll perfume the Air a little. [*Besprinkles him with the Bottle*]

ANDROB. Hold, Sirrah, hold. Well, if I were alive they durst not have us'd me thus; This usage convinces me more then any thing else. [*Exit*]

[173]

TOM. He has it, he has it; I doubt it will be a hard matter to persuade him to Life again.

Act Third, Scene Third
Enter FIZLE *and* FLIP.

FIZLE. We see, *Tom,* you are very busy. But if it be no Interruption, pray give us leave to ask you, In what manner the General is to make his Entry?

TOM. . . . Rest you Merry, Gentlemen. [*Exit*]

FIZLE. We shall learn nothing from this Fellow; but so far we know, that the Keeper must assist at it; And from a broad by hints we have understood, that if he is destroy'd any how, so the General be not seen in't, He'll take that Trust upon himself; Then all will be well. Now if we can but Contrive to have the Chair over Loaded, plac'd Upon the Hatch over the Vault, and the Hatch Unbolted, or so weakly Barr'd, that its weight may sink him Down, we shall get Rid of him, and it will appear to the world to be the meer Effect of Chance.

TOM. [*Peeping*] Are you there with your Bears? I shall be up with you. I'll go find out *Solemn,* and try to build on this Foundation of their own Laying. [*Exit*]

FLIP. This is Admirable, and cannot fail; Let's loose no time, but go about it streight; I'll get into the Vault, and Prepare the Bolt; do you take care to place the Chair. Here comes old *Solemn;* no more words, but *Mumm.* [*Exeunt. Enter* SOLEMN *and* TOM]

SOLEMN. Are you sure that you heard distinctly? The Excess of the Villainy makes it incredible!

TOM. Am I sure that I live? But if you doubt it, the very Tampering with the Chair will Convince you.

SOLEMN. Away then, acquaint the Keeper, and *AEsop,* leave the rest to me. One thing you must take care be Punctually Observ'd, that is, That *Androboros* Friends be planted next to the Chair, by way of Precedency. Quick, Quick, be gone. . . . Here he comes pat. *Nick-Nack,* How dos't do? I'm glad to see thee Awake with all my heart.

[174]

ANDROB. Is the Dev'l in the Fellow? He can see me now without the Help of his Gymcrack; not to mention your odd Familiarity. What d'ye mean by Awake? When was I asleep?

SOLEMN. Asleep! You have been so Time out of mind. You have been Walking asleep, Talking asleep, and Fighting asleep, I know not how long.

ANDROB. I'm glad it's no worse; I Thought I was Dead, at least every body else seem'd to think so.

SOLEMN. Dead! No, No; it is all a Jest.

ANDROB. Why, you old Raskal, you, Did you but now start at the sight of me, as if you had seen a Ghost?

SOLEMN. True; yet you are not actually Dead, but Invisible to all the World besides, and must continue so, so long as I shall think fitting.

ANDROB. [*Aside*] I ever thought this Fellow had the black Art. [*To him*] I wish thou would'st change that Curse for any other. Canst thou not make thy self invisible to me, as thou hast done me to other Folks? So far I own I would be oblig'd to thee, and thank thee.

SOLEMN. If that will oblige you, 'tis done, Look but into this Telescope, and in that instant I shall become invisible to you. [*Looks into a hollow Cane;* SOLEMN *from the other End blows Snuff into his Eyes*] It is done?

ANDROB. Villain, Dog, Raskal, I'm blind; Where are ye, ye Villain. Murderer?

SOLEMN. Here, This way, This way; You must see with your Ears, until I shall think fit to unsear your Eyes, General; That is the bargain, if I remember right. [*Exit* SOLEMN, ANDROB. *Groping his way after him*]

Act Third, Scene Fourth
Curtain drawn, Discovers KEEPER, DEPUTY, TOM, ÆSOP, FIZLE, FLIP, COXCOMB, BABILARD, MULLEGRUB, &c.

KEEPER. Let the Black Gentlemen be Rank'd as they desire; I'll do all I can to please e'm.

[175]

ÆSOP. With all my Heart, Only I thought it bad Hearldry that these who are supported by the Chair, should support it.

KEEPER. Another time you shall have your way; I'll have it so now; Let the Rest observe their distance. [*Here they are rank'd,* FIZLE *and* FLIP *next to the Chair*]

ÆSOP. I'll keep as distant as I can, that I may be at Ease; *FIZLE'S* Phiz always gives me the Chollick. . . . And first of the First.

Nature, which nothing leaves to Chance,
    Had dealt to Creatures of each Kind,
Provision for their Sustenance,
      To some her Bounty had Assign'd
        The Herb o'th' Fields, whilst others had
        The Spoils of Trees, but All were Fed.

The Grunting Kind obtain'd the last,
    A happy Lot; for every Wood
Afforded store of Nuts and Mast,
      And *Joves* own Tree did Show'r down Food
        Enough for all, could all his Store
        Have kept that Herb from Craving more.

But they with Sloath and Plenty Cloy'd,
    Wax'd Wanton, and with Tusks Profane,
First, all the sacred Trees Destroy'd,
      Which fed 'em; Next invade the Plain,
        Where harmless Flocks did graze, and Spoil
        With Rav'nous Snouts the fertile Soil.

Jove hears the loud Complaints and Cry's
    Of Suff'ring Flocks, and streight Ordains,
That hence-forth Hogs be pen't in Sty's,
      And fed with Wash, and Husks, and Grains,

[176]

Where ever since th' Unhallow'd Race
Wallows in Fat and Filthyness.

. . .

ANDROB. [*Within*] I'll have the Villain Hang'd; Dog, Raskal, Rogue, Scoundrel.

ÆSOP. By my Life, it is the General making his Entry; It seems he has got no Herald for this Triumph, that he thus Proclaims his own Titles. [*Enter* SOLEMN, ANDROBOROS *following him*]

SOLEMN. Make way there, Make way; Room, Room for the General. This Way,—This way—[SOLEMN *Steps aside*, AN-DROBOROS *Runs blindly upon the Chair*, FIZLE *and* FLIP *Endeavouring to Stop him, Sink with Him*]

FIZLE and FLIP. Hold, Hold; Help! Help! Help!

KEEPER. What's the meaning of this?

SOLEMN. 'Tis but a Trap of their Own laid for you, Sir, in which They Themselves are Caught.

COXCOMB. Let's be done! There is no Safety here. [COXCOM. BABILARD, MULLIGRUB *Sneaking off*]

SOLEMN. What! You are making your Retreat; you need not fear, you are a sort of Vermin not worth the Bait; The others have their Deserts.

> *In former Ages virtuous Deeds*
> *Rais'd Mortals to the blest Abodes,*
> *But Hero's of the Mode(r)n Breed*
> *And Saints go downward to the Gods.*

[*Exeunt*]

Curtain Falls
FINIS

[177]

PROVINCIAL NEWSPAPER WIT

THE colonial newspapers have been tantalizing and frustrating scholars of early American culture for years. They can provide a wealth of information about colonial life, but only if one is willing to weather the long reiterations of European affairs which dominated most issues. In this regard the newspapers were vital in counteracting North American provincialism, for without such information, colonists would have been more poorly informed about the rest of the world. As it was, they were only six months to one year behind major continental developments. Moreover, there was a real, if limited, coverage of intercolonial events which helped forge whatever common identity the provincials came to share. Advertisements, particularly for run-away slaves in the South,[1] reveal valuable data on economic and social behavior, but the fact remains that the newspapers were primarily directed at European affairs and to the urban colonial reader. As such, they are deeply disappointing for those looking for wilderness life and laughter.

Governmental censorship further limited the richness of newspaper sources, and the colonial divisions over gubernatorial or legislative dominance simply added to the number of possible reasons for censorship. If the printer had cleared his copy with the governor and then the legislators, there was still the ever-sensitive reading public to assuage. As the leading expert on the subject put it,

As long as the printer of the colonies executed his work correctly and, in

1. For example: Gerald Mullin, *Flight and Rebellion: Slave Resistance in Eighteenth Century Virginia* (New York: Oxford University Press, 1972).

[178]

the vulgar phrase, kept a civil tongue in his head, he was free from interference . . . It was easy, however, to make a slip. . . .[2]

In this atmosphere, the newspapers produced little humor of high originality and even less of a biting, rebellious nature. The pieces which follow are amusing but very, very safe: Anonymity is preserved, governmental subjects avoided or gingerly juggled, and the unique wilderness surroundings studiously blocked out. Indeed, one obvious theme of newspaper humor is its overt juxtaposition of urban sophistication with country naivete. When attention is diverted occasionally from the comedy of manners to the rural or frontier theme, readers enjoyed a comforting laugh at the backcountry. In the more positive sense, readers were treated to a voyeuristic giggle about the sexual playgrounds of provincial urbanity.   W. H. K.

The New England Courant, January 29, 1722[3]

Several Journeymen Gentlemen, (Some Foreigners and others of our own Growth) never sully'd with Business, and fit for Town or Country Diversion, are willing to dispose of themselves in Marriage as follows: *VIZ.* Some to old Virgins, who by long Industry have laid up £500 or prov'd themselves capable of maintaining a Husband in a genteel and commendable Idleness. Some to old or young Widows who have Estates of their first Husbands getting, to dispose of at their second Husbands Pleasure. And some to young Ladies under Age, who have their Fortunes in their own Hands, and are willing to maintain a pretty genteel Man, rather than be without him.

2. Lawrence C. Wroth, *The Colonial Printer* (Portland, Me.: Southworth-Anthoensen Press, 1938), pp. 175–77. Wroth notes a "rowdy but amuzing piece, *The Isle of Pines,*" was prohibited in 1668 in Massachusetts.
3. Contributed to the *William and Mary Quarterly,* XII, 4 (Oct. 1955), 651 by Philip Detweiler.

N. B. The above Gentlemen may be spoke with almost any Hour in the Day, at the Tick-Tavern in Prodigal Square, and will proceed to Courtship as soon as their Mistresses shall pay their Tavern Scores.

New York Weekly Journal, December 31, 1733

We hear from Ridgefield, near the Country of Westchester, that one *William Drinkwater,* late an Inhabitant there proveing quarrelsom with his Neighbours and abusing to his Wife, the good Women of the Place, took the Matter into Consideration and laid hold of an Opportunity, to get him tied to a Cart, and there with Rods belaboured him on his Back, till, in striving to get away, he pulled one of his Arms out of Joint, and then they unti'd him. Mr. *Drinkwater* complained to sundrie Magistrates of this useage, but all he got by it was to be Laughed at; Whereupon he removed to *New-Milford* where we hear he proves a good Neighbour and a loveing Husband. *A remarkable Reformation ariseing from the Justice of the good Women.*

New York Weekly Journal, March 25, 1734

Philadelphia, March 12

We hear from Matfield in Bucks County, that on *Shrove Tuesday* last one *James Worthington,* after having eaten a hearty Meal of Beef and Pork, eat Forty one and a half boil'd Hens Eggs, and would have eaten more if some in Company had not taken them from him; he eat Bread and Salt plentifully with them, and said he could have eaten Ten more. He was not in the least Disordered with his Dinner, but eat a very hearty Supper about 5 or 6 Hours after.

New York Weekly Journal, July 15, 1734

Philadelphia, July 11. On the 6th Instant at Bybery, one *James*

[180]

Worthington, as he was reaping was so overcome with the excessive Heat of the Weather that he felldown, those about him removed him into the Shade, in Hopes that he would recover, but in vain, for he died immediately.

N. B. He was the Person mentioned in our Journal of the 25th of March last that eat 41 and a half hard boil'd Hens Eggs after a hearty Diner.

New York Weekly Journal, June 3, 1734

New York, June 3d.

Last week one *Thomas Copley,* was apprehended here, on Suspicion of Coining and uttering false Dollars, when he found himself discover'd he flung 18 in a Purse over the Fence into a Neighbouring Yard, some that he kept loose in his Pocket he dropt into the Privy, the Purse was immediately found but it is supposed that those which he dropt into the Privy are not all found.

Boston *Weekly News-Letter,* March 20, 1735[4]

A young Gentleman of Durham in Connecticut, had addressed a Lady in the Neighborhood with his solemn Protestations of Love, and asked for an approving Smile, and continued very Fervant in his Courtship, for about Two Years last past: But the young Woman, conscious of her superior Merit, always appeared with a forbidding Frown: This at last so discouraged the fond Courtier, that he gave over the pursuit; but being restless, he applys to his Father for Relief, by his kind Mediation; and he, being willing to help his favourite Son in this difficult Case, immediately mounts his Horse and away, to the Parents of the young Woman; and discoursing half an Hour with them, they agree and strike up a Match: The young Man being informed hereof, was so overcome

4. Contributed to the *William and Mary Quarterly,* XXIII, 2 (April 1966), 309–10 by Howard H. Peckham.

[181]

with a sudden Joy, that he grew delirious, in which Frame he continued three Days, when it was termed Distraction: Hereon a Doctor was sent for, who coming, inquired the Cause, and finding it to be Love, he ordered the young Woman to be sent for, she came accordingly, and found her Captive raving: The sight of her revived him, and partly restored him, so much as enabled him to desire her to sit down; which done, he laid his Head on her Bosom, and slept for about an Hour and then awoke; but such sudden Raptures of Joy returning, proved strong for his Imagination, and losing the government of his Passions, in superextatick Joy made his Exit.

New York Weekly Journal, May 5, 1735

Philadelphia, April 17
   We hear from Chester County, that last Week at a Vendue held there, a Man being unreasonably abusive to his Wife upon some trifling Occasion, the Women form'd themselves into a Court, and ordered him to be apprehended by their Officers and brought to Tryal: Being found guilty he was condemn'd to be duck'd 3 Times in a neighbouring Pond, and to have one half cut off, of his Hair and Beard (which it seems he wore at full length) and the Sentence was accordingly executed, to the great Diversion of the Spectators.

New York Weekly Journal, November 8, 1736

Boston, November 1
   On Saturday Evening the 23d Instant, one *Ezekiel N —d—m* of this Town, and another Young Man that formerly lived with Mr. *P—rs—n's* of this Town, was going over to Roxbury, to see their Mistresses, were met between the Fortification and the Gallows by a Troop of young Ladies or Female Foot Pads [Highwaymen], who instantly surrounded them and attacked them, but *Ezekiel* by reason of his very long Legs soon Straddled out of their Reach, but left the other unhappy Man a sacrifice to their Rage, who immediately seized him, and threw him down to the Ground, and

some holding him fast, the others strip'd down his Breeches and whip'd him most unmercifully; but *Ezekiel* got off without any Damage, saving he was very much affrighted.

New York Weekly Journal, January 19, 1736

We hear from the borders of *Tweed,* that a certain Tonsor [barber], brimful of Courage, went out to attack a Highwayman; and in the Heighth of the Fury of his Pursuit, he narrowly escaped dashing out his own Brains against a Post.

South-Carolina Gazette, September 6, 1735

On Monday Evening last, Capt. ——— lately Master of a Sloop, and a young *Tonsor* of this Town, had a mind to imitate your Gentlemen of Honour, by a Trial of Skill at Sword and Pistol, wherein they rather frightened than hurt each other; and the most melancholy Circumstance attending this hardy Adventure, is, that Capt. *Quixot* has since fainted away several times from a strong Imagination of himself being mortally wounded, and having actually killed his Antagonist. This grand Quarrel, like most others of that sort, unhappily arose from their several Pretensions to the Favours of a certain sable Beauty. . . .

> Two Hotspurs unnoted for martial adventures,
> To give the World proof they were right bully ranters,
> Talk'd big to each other of prowess and fighting,
> Tho' some say, their breeches more savour'd of sh—ng
> Yet out they both turn'd, and to battle they went,
> Both lug'd out their Swords, and began to—repent:
> When each by consent, fear of rusting his blade,
> Made his scabbard receive all the thrusts that were made,
> Then freely shook hands, greatly griev'd they had flouted,
> And so return'd home like Two Heroes redoubted

Thus oft have I seen two dunghill cocks meet,
With crests high erect, peck and scrape with their feet
Then instead of advancing both draw off and crow,
And strut to their hens without one sparring blow.

New York Weekly Journal, February 9, 1736

Fairfield (Connecticut), Feb. 3

Mr. Zenger,

After a long Debate between two Men, one of *New-England,* and the other of *New-York,* concerning which of their Magistrates acted most uprightly, they fell into the following Discourse, the Persons present were *Deacon Cannon* and *John Panther.*

Deacon Cannon. I wonder Mr. *Panther* you pretend to justifie your Magistrates.

Panther. I think they can be justified:

D. Yes, if wickedness is any Justification, it may be done.

P. *Tell me one of our Country Magistrates that have acted wrongly.*

D. I'll begin with Justice *Sweetwell.*

P. *What of him?*

D. He was once upon a Time at a Barbicue Shote [Shoat] where, when he had fed heartily, he was overtaken in a fit of Love.

P. *You're mistaken, he only went to feed her with some of the Fragments out of Charity, for he is a charitable Man.*

D. That can't be, for she was well fed before: But these are Trifles. I know this same Judge *Sweetwell,* being appointed one of the Judges to try a Criminal, had in his Shoes a pair of Buckles that he had got from the said Criminal.

P. *What of that, he got them by a fair Truck.*

D. Never a bit the Honester for that: But there is the Sheep Pasture.

P. *That's an old Story, and a Ewe Lamb can blind some Peoples Eyes.*

D. What do you think of Judge *Sweetwell's* ordering the said Criminal to be Transported to Avoid Justice.

[184]

P. *Good Reason, to prevent further Inquiries.*
D. If these be your Country Judges, Deliver me from them!

New York Weekly Journal, March 1, 1736

New York, Feb. 25, 1735-6
   Mr. *Zenger:*
     I am one of those that have always thought that there is a certain Chearfulness and Vivacity in the Conversation of the fair Sex, not to be found in our own, and therefore it has usually been my Custom, after the busy Hours of the Day are over, to seek a Dish of Tea with some one of my Female Acquaintance; I am happy in two or three, who, as they know my Humour, are pleas'd to tell me, I shall be always wellcome: Accordingly I went the other Day to Mrs. ———, expecting to have found only one or two Intimates, but upon entering the Room was surprized with a very large Company of agreeable Women, between the Ages of fifteen and fifty. For some little Time after I came in, there appeared as much Silence as was necessary to inform me that I was not expected; however, after having made my Complements and taken a Chair, one of my good Friends reasumed the Discourse, saying, I might be useful to them, in acting the Part of their Secretary, for that they were about to ask your Advice in an Affair of Liberty and Importance. You will easily believe I was a little vain of this new Employment, and with some of my best Phrase, I returned the Ladies Thanks for the Honour they did me. Pen, Ink & Paper being brought the Mistress of the House took the great Chair, and very methodically proposed, that the Ladies should seperately dictate such Queries as they thought necessary for your Advice; and these were as follows.
    Mrs. ——— a Maiden Lady, of middle Age, says She hears there is a Meeting which is kept on every *Tuesday* Evening, at four certain Houses in this City, which is called *The* HUNC OVER DE *Club;* but having ever been cautious of her Character, and not knowing what is meant by the Game of HUNC OVER DE, for she

[185]

understands it is a Sport, prays you will explain it to her, and advise her as to her Conduct herein.

Mrs. ———, a Widow of about Five and Thirty, says, she has made the best Enquiry she has been able about the said HUNC OVER DE *Club,* and that, as it is described to her, there is no Difficulty in their Sport but what may be soon acquired, that she conceives she understands it well, and proposes another Society of *Hunc over de's* to be established by the Company present, with a competent Number of Males, but submits it to your Advice, and the Opinion of the younger Ladies, for the Elder she thinks are less interested in the Matter.

Mrs. ——— an English Lady of full Age, says she has been acquainted with many People of Quality and of lower Stations, and has played at most Games with them, that she never heard of any by the Name of *Hunc Over De,* that she is not learned enough to determine what Language this Game is taken from, but she suspects it to be *Jewish,* or *Rabbinical,* and as she is a great Lover of the Church, cannot agree to it, but desires whatever Game is established, it may have a more *Arthodox* Name. —

Miss. ——— a young Lady of agreeable Person, who thinks by a very ridiculous piece of Coprice she has been excluded from being one of the *Hunc over De's* already established, desires to return Thanks for her lucky Escape, but she at the same Time declares she is ready in an *Orthodox* Manner to be as merry as any Body, and hopes you will advise the young Gentlemen of the Town, to think more of their Belles and less of their Bottles.

Several other Questions were started, ——— but an unexpected visitor of the *Hunc Over De* Party, occasioned an Adjournment, and I was ordered to transmit there immediately to you, . . .

Your Humble Servant,
Trusty Roger

Direct for me at the Sign of the Torn-Gown and Towsled Headcloaths near the Bowling-Green.

[186]

New York Weekly Journal, May 16, 1737

Mr. Zenger,
  Being the other Day at ——— I was presented with the copy
of a Will of one ——— Solom, which being somewhat comical, be
pleased to insert in your next . . .

     TO thee my Spouse,
     I leave my House,
   Which sadly wants repairing;
      Nine Quarts of Pease,
      Some Candle Grease,
   A well made handsome Earring.

     Two wooden Loggs,
     Two mastiff Dogs,
   Old Cringer and Come-hither;
      A Crust of Cheese,
      Two Apple Trees,
   With an old Stepless Ladder:

     Five half hatch'd Eggs,
     Eight Cedar Peggs,
   A Tap and broken Fasset,
      Three Yards of Twine,
      Some Apple Wine,
   A Pen and Ink, Jove bless it.

     A Pair of Shoes,
     Whose Heels and Toes,
   Long since my Dear are worn out;
      A Batter'd Jugg
      An Earthen Mugg
   Alas! but nought to pour out.

[187]

Of Calves ten Tail
Two broken Rails,
A well made wooden Cleaver,
Which neighbour Jone
Will have her own,
But my Dear don't believe her.

A leaking Pail
A crooked Nail,
Three Quarters of a Rye Bread.
Two holy Books
To frighten spooks,
Which oft has rais'd my Eye-Lids.

The World I'm sure,
Will you endure,
If you are worth all these Things;
(For)
If all were sold,
And turned to Gold,
Its worth would be two Knee-Strings.[5]

Virginia Gazette, July 28, 1738[6]

Last week a Team of five Horses and a Waggon with 2500 Weight of Tea, was seiz'd near Chichester in Sussex, by two Custom-house Officers, assisted by a Guard of Soldiers.

On Sunday last, Mr. Forster, Surveyor-General of the River, seiz'd a considerable Quantity of Tea at Woolwich, hid under some Hoop-Petticoats. The Owners of those Goods could be no experienced Smugglers, as is plain by their Choice of so improper a Place for Concealment, the Custom-House Officers being generally re-

5. Strings worn around the knees at the bottom of knee-breeches.
6. *William and Mary Quarterly,* IX, 4 (Oct. 1952), 543.

markable for having a natural Itch to rummage under Petticoats.
——— For, some time since, A Custom-House Officer being in
the Pit at the Play-house, went to put his Hands up one of the
Orange Wenches Petticoats, but the Girl knew him, and cry'd out,
How, now, Mr. Tide-Waiter, there is nothing there *but what has
been fairly Enter'd*.

The American Magazine and Historical Chronicle (Boston,
November 1743)

To the publishers
Gentlemen.

I have lately been reading the histories of those renowned War-
riors of Greece . . . Their courage, Conduct and success have
inspired me with an ardent love of fame, and my thirst after it is so
unquenchable that I am determined to raise a reputation that shall
shine in future Annals and distinguish my name and family in the
records of distant ages: Methinks I see the name *Weatherwise*
already advanced to the Pinnacle of Honour and my *dear Country*
erecting Statues and Pyramids to the man who exalted it to that
pitch of Glory now approaching. Indians innumerable I have
destroyed, which would have immortalized my fame, but by ne-
glecting to bring hom their scalps, I have therefore been secluded
from a *Gazette* or *Post Boy*[7] (for I have no witnesses to my
Heroism) and so have lost my triumph.

Turning instead to astrology   The next Prognostick is that of the
Goose Bone: In proportion to the Blackness of it, so will the
severity of the season be . . . The only way to be just in this
observation, is to keep a close look to the following rules, viz. The
Goose must be a wild one; hatched in the Month of May, and killed
with *Swan* shot on the 27th of *September;* when the breast-bone is
well cleansed from the flesh, you must calculate from the forepart
of it and so on towards the tail part: Some Persons indeed begin at
the tail part and go back towards the forepart, but you may as well
imagine *February* to happen before *December* as to calculate in

---

7. Newspapers, as in The Boston *Post Boy*.

that manner. I should have communicated my sentiments upon this *Sign,* with regard to this Winter, but the Man I had engaged to kill me a *Goose,* was confined by the Gout, so that the Publick must suffer by his Misfortune.

South Carolina Gazette, March 20, 1749

A RHAPSODY on RUM

GREAT Spirit hail—Confusion's angry Sire,
And like thy Parent *Bacchus,* born of Fire:
The Goal's Decoy; the greedy Merchant's Lure;
Disease of Money, but Reflection's Cure.

We owe great DRAM! the trembling Hand to thee,
The headstrong Purpose; and the feeble Knee;
The Loss of Honour; and the Cause of Wrong;
The Brain enchanted; and the faultering Tongue;
Whilst Fancy flies before Thee unconfin'd,
Thou leav'st disabled Prudence far behind.

In thy Pursuit our Fields are left forlorn,
Whilst giant Weeds oppress the pigmy Corn:
Thou throw'st a Mist before the Planter's Eyes;
The Plough grows idle, and the Harvest dies.

By Thee refresh'd no cruel Norths we fear;
'Tis ever warm and calm when thou art near:
On the bare Earth for Thee expos'd we lie,
And brave the Malice of a weeping Skie.
And seem like those that did of old repent;
We sit in Ashes, and our Cloathes are rent.

From Thee a thousand flatt'ring Whims escape,
Like hasty Births, that ne'er have perfect Shape.

[190]

Thine Ideots seem in gay Delusion fair,
But born in Flame, they soon expire in Air.

O grand Deluder! such thy charming Art,
'Twere good we ne'er should meet, or ne'er should part:
Ever abscond, or ever tend our Call;
Leave us our Sense, or none at all.

J. DUMBLETON

Boston Gazette, May 5, 1755[8]

One Day last Week, a strapping Country Fellow was leading his Horse with his Hands behind him down the Long Wharff; and as he pass'd by the T, an unlucky Sailor slipt the Bridle from the Horse's Head, and plac'd it on his own, leaving the Horse and two Panniards [baskets] of Apples to his Mess Mate, to be properly taken care of, who soon conceal'd them. — The Countryman after leading the Tar some considerable Way, turn'd about, and, to his great Consternation, found in the Room of his Horse, the Appearance of a Man. — The Sailor observing the Confusion in the Countryman's Face, with a very serious compos'd Countenance, addressed him in the following Words. *My good Master,* I would not have you be surpriz'd at this strange Appearance, for Things now turn out exactly agreeable to the Prediction of my old Grandmother. — This Grandmother of mine was a Witch—and taking Offence at me about seven Years ago, transmogrifyed me into a Horse; but for my Comfort, told me, that in such a Time, I should be releas'd, and resume my old Form of Existence—which Times is out this Day, and accordingly I am now changed from an Horse to a Man. The Countryman finding himself jockey'd, and the People by this Time crowding around him, told the Sailor, If he would return him the Horse, he was welcome to his Load: The Horse presently appear'd without the Panniards—the Fellow mounted and rode up the Wharff as fast as he could drive.

8. *William and Mary Quarterly,* XXV, 3 (July 1968), 475.

[191]

THE BOURGEOIS HUMOR

OF

BENJAMIN FRANKLIN

BENJAMIN Franklin (1706–1790) has provided both the points of departure and conclusion in most thinking about colonial American humor. The touches of wit with which he adorned his widely-read *Autobiography*[1] linger on in the American imagination. Indeed, Franklin's wit is an important ingredient in the usual image of the sly sage and founding father. Testimony to this enduring popularity is found in such books as *Ben Franklin's Wit & Wisdom,*[2] which presents Franklin's borrowed and "adapted" sayings to the general reading public.

Franklin had a fine sense of humor, so this reputation is justified. Much of his comic success rested upon his skill with words. His "wise sayings" provoke laughter from our surprise at the contrast and economy of his word-play. "Neither a Fortress nor a Maidenhead will hold out long after they begin to parley;" and "In Marriage without love, there will be Love without Marriage," are typical of Franklin's facility in turning few words to comic effect. In addition, the combination of sober sagacity with a slyness of wit enhances our pleasure in its unexpectedness. The oracle winks and we laugh at the realization that the joke is partly on us.

Franklin's humor is greatly dependent upon his play with masks and roles. In *Anthony Afterwit,* for example, we develop an image of a poor clod who has been duped by his own petty greed into a marriage with an expensive woman. Just as we begin to lament this depressing situation, the tables begin to turn and Anthony enjoys

1. Leonard W. Labaree *et al.,* eds., *The Autobiography of Benjamin Franklin* (New Haven: Yale University Press, 1964).
2. Mount Vernon, N.Y.: Peter Pauper Press, n.d.

the last laugh on his wife and on us. We marvel at the skill with which Franklin has woven a moral lesson into a comic story. The same mechanism works with no little success in his advice to a marriage-shy bachelor. After setting us up with a straight-faced sermon on the sanctity of marriage, Franklin reverses form and lists reasons and ways to avoid it. He tricks his readers in revealing his awareness of the contrasts between appearance and reality.

Franklin's slyness, his sleight-of-hand, and his cleverness with words are impressive, but mark the limits of his comic spirit as well. According to his *Autobiography,* which is close to "the longest covert and sustained joke" in American History,[3] Franklin learned early in his life that his penchant for iconoclastic witticisms was offensive to those who prized conventional wisdom.[4] Because he prized community leadership and esteem, Franklin cultivated what he called a "Socratic Method" in social interchange. According to this approach, he hid his sentiments under a mask of gravity, while limiting his intellectual and comic rebelliousness to private enjoyment. It would not do to reveal the comic absurdity which he found in contemporary social and religious customs.

As a result, Franklin's humor is quite tame when compared with that of George Alsop or Ebenezer Cook. The laughter which he directed at social pretensions and follies was limited to neutral subjects like eating, drinking, marriage, and ambition. One strongly suspects that his sense of humor was profound and extraordinarily revolutionary, for Franklin questioned the basic institutions of his society. He chose, nevertheless, to conceal any insights which might be found unacceptable and, more importantly, paraded himself as a bastion of respectability.

Franklin's cultivation of social respectability led him as far away from the American wilderness as he could get. He wanted to overcome the primitive, frontier stage of development and leap into the coming world of science and European culture. While in Philadelphia, he dedicated himself to leading the city into the modern age and during his long residence in England and France he

3. Bier, *The Rise and Fall of American Humor,* p. 49.
4. *Autobiography,* pp. 64–65, 88, 96, 114, 150, 165.

surrounded himself with the brightest lights of European culture and intellectuality. One will look in vain for any recognition of the forests, the Indians, wild animals or the like in Franklin's humorous writings before the revolution. His laughter was in the wilderness but not of it. One can only guess why, but his "bagatelle" from Passy about the "Savages" of North America hints that Franklin saw quite clearly the cruelty of the joke which he had helped play on a virgin land. If the Indians were not really *savages* and Anglo-American culture was not, after all, truly *civilized,* then it would be more appropriate to cry than to laugh. That dilemma was cosmic and Franklin seems to have dismissed it in his efforts to invent a more perfect world.

W.H.K.

To the Author of the *New-England Courant* [May 14, 1722]

Sir,

Discoursing the other Day at Dinner with my Reverend Boarder, formerly mention'd, (whom for Distinction sake we will call by the Name of Clericus,) concerning the Education of Children, I ask'd his advice about my young Son William, whether or no I had best bestow upon him Academical Learning, or (as our Phrase is) *bring him up at our College:* He perswaded me to do it by all Means, using many weighty Arguments with me, and answering all the Objections that I could form against it; . . .

As soon as Dinner was over, I took a solitary Walk into my Orchard, still ruminating on Clericus's Discourse with much Consideration, until I came to my usual Place of Retirement under the *Great Apple-Tree;* where having seated my self, and carelessly laid my Head on a verdant Bank, I fell by Degrees into a soft and undisturbed Slumber. My waking Thoughts remained with me in my Sleep, and before I awak'd again, I dreamt the following DREAM.

I fancy'd I was travelling over pleasant and delightful Fields and Meadows, and thro' many small Country Towns and Villages; and as I pass'd along, all Places resounded with the Fame of the Temple of LEARNING: Every Peasant, who had wherewithal, was preparing to send one of his Children at least to this famous Place; and in this Case most of them consulted their own Purses instead of their Childrens Capacities: So that I observed, a great many, yea, the most part of those who were travelling thither, were little better than Dunces and Blockheads. Alas! Alas!

At length I entred upon a spacious Plain, in the Midst of which was erected a large and stately Edifice: It was to this that a great Company of Youths from all Parts of the Country were going; so stepping in among the Crowd, I passed on with them, and presently arrived at the Gate.

The Passage was kept by two sturdy Porters named *Riches* and *Poverty,* and the latter obstinately refused to give Entrance to any who had not first gain'd Favour of the former; so that I observed, many who came even to the very Gate, were obliged to travel back again as ignorant as they came, for want of this necessary Qualification. However, as a Spectator I gain'd Admittance, and with the rest entred directly into the Temple.

In the Middle of the great Hall stood a stately and magnificent Throne, which was ascended to by two high and difficult Steps. On the Top of it sat LEARNING in awful State; she was apparelled wholly in Black, and surrounded almost on every Side with innumerable Volumes in all Languages. She seem'd very busily employ'd in writing something on half a Sheet of Paper, and upon Enquiry, I understood she was preparing a Paper, call'd, *The New-England Courant.* On her Right Hand sat *English,* with a pleasant smiling Countenance, and handsomely attir'd; and on her left were seated several *Antique Figures* with their Faces vail'd. I was considerably puzzl'd to guess who they were, until one informed me, (who stood by me,) that those Figures on her left Hand were *Latin, Greek, Hebrew,* &c. and that they were very much reserv'd, and seldom or never unvail'd their Faces here, and then to few or none, tho' most of those who have in this Place acquir'd so much Learning as to distinguish them from *English,* pretended to an intimate Acquaintance with them. I then enquir'd of him, what could be the

[195]

Reason why they continued vail'd, in this Place especially: He pointed to the Foot of the Throne, where I saw *Idleness,* attended with *Ignorance,* and there (he informed me) were they, who first vail'd them, and still kept them so.

Now I observed, that the whole Tribe who entred into the Temple with me, began to climb the Throne; but the Work proving troublesome and difficult to most of them, they withdrew their Hands from the Plow, and contented themselves to sit at the Foot, with Madam *Idleness* and her Maid *Ignorance,* until those who were assisted by Diligence and a docible Temper, had well nigh got up the first Step: But the Time drawing nigh in which they could no way avoid ascending, they were fain to crave the Assistance of those who had got up before them, and who, for the Reward perhaps of a *Pint of Milk,* or a *Piece of Plumb-Cake,*[5] lent the Lubbers a helping Hand, and sat them in the Eye of the World, upon a Level with themselves.

The Other Step being in the same Manner ascended, and the usual Ceremonies at an End, every Beetle-Scull [numbskull] seem'd well satisfy'd with his own Portion of Learning, tho' perhaps he was *e'en just* as ignorant as ever. And now the Time of their Departure being come, they march'd out of Doors to make Room for another Company, who waited for Entrance: And I, having seen all that was to be seen, quitted the Hall likewise, and went to make my Observations on those who were just gone out before me.

Some I perceiv'd took to Merchandizing, others to Travelling, some to one Thing, some to another, and some to Nothing; and many of them from henceforth, for want of Patrimony, liv'd as poor as Church Mice, being unable to dig, asham'd to beg, and to live by their Wits was impossible. But the most Part of the Crowd went along a large beaten Path, which led to a Temple at the further End of the Plain, call'd, *The Temple of Theology.* The Business of those who were employ'd in this Temple being laborious and painful, I wonder'd exceedingly to see so many go towards it; but while I was pondering this Matter in my Mind, I spy'd *Pecunia* behind a Curtain, beckoning to them with her Hand, which Sight im-

5. A traditional treat at Harvard on graduation day.

[196]

mediately satisfy'd me for whose Sake it was, that a great Part of them (I will not say all) travel'd that Road. In this Temple I saw nothing worth mentioning, except the ambitious and fraudulent Contrivances of Plagius, who (notwithstanding he had been severely reprehended for such Practices before) was diligently transcribing some eloquent Paragraphs out of Tillotson's *Works,* &c., to embellish his own.

Now I bethought to my self in my Sleep, that it was Time to be Home, and as I fancy'd I was travelling back thither, I reflected in my Mind on the extream Folly of those Parents, who, blind to their Children's Dulness, and insensible of the Solidity of their Skulls, because they think their Purses can afford it, will needs send them to the Temple of Learning, where, for want of a suitable Genius, they learn little more than how to carry themselves handsomely, and enter a Room genteely, (which might as well be acquir'd at a Dancing-School,) and from whence they return, after Abundance of Trouble and Charge, as great Blockheads as ever, only more proud and self-conceited.

While I was in the midst of these unpleasant Reflections, Clericus (who with a Book in his Hand was walking under the Trees) accidentally awak'd me; to him I related my Dream with all its Particulars, and he, without much Study, presently interpreted it, assuring me, *That it was a lively Representation* of HARVARD COLLEGE, Etcetera. I remain, Sir, Your Humble Servant,

SILENCE DOGOOD

Anthony Afterwit
(from the *Pennsylvania Gazette,* July 10, 1732)

Mr. Gazetteer,
I am an honest Tradesman, who never meant Harm to any Body.
My Affairs went on smoothly while a Batchelor; but of late I have

met with some Difficulties, of which I take the Freedom to give you an Account.

About the Time I first address'd my present Spouse, her Father gave out in Speeches, that if she married a Man he liked, he would give with her £200 on the Day of Marriage. 'Tis true he never said so to me, but he always receiv'd me very kindly at his House, and openly countenanc'd my Courtship. I form'd several fine Schemes, what to do with this same £200 and in some Measure neglected my Business on that Account: But unluckily it came to pass, that when the old Gentleman saw I was pretty well engag'd, and that the Match was too far gone to be easily broke off; he, without any Reason given, grew very angry, forbid me the House, and told his Daughter that if she married me he would not give her a Farthing. However (as he forsaw) we were not to be disappointed in that Manner; but having stole a Wedding, I took her home to my House; where we were not in quite so poor a Condition as the Couple describ'd in the Scotch Song, who had

> *Neither Pot nor Pan,*
> *But four bare Legs together;*

for I had a House tolerably furnished, for an ordinary Man, before. No thanks to Dad, who I understand was very much pleased with his politick Management. And I have since learn'd that there are old Curmudgeons (*so called*) besides him, who have this Trick, to marry their Daughters, and yet keep what they might well spare, till they can keep it no longer: But this by way of Digression; *A Word to the Wise is enough.*

I soon saw that with Care and Industry we might live tolerably easy, and in Credit with our Neighbours: But my Wife had a strong Inclination to be a *Gentle-woman.* In consequence of this, my old-fashioned Looking-Glass was one Day broke, as she said, *No Mortal could tell which way.* However, since we could not be without a Glass in the Room, *My Dear,* says she, *we may as well buy a large fashionable One that Mr. Such-a-one has to sell; it will cost but little more than a common Glass, and will be much handsomer and more creditable.* Accordingly the Glass was bought, and hung against the Wall: But in a Week's time, I was

[198]

made sensible by little and little, *that the Table was by no Means suitable to such a Glass*. And a more proper Table being procur'd, my Spouse, who was an excellent Contriver, inform'd me where we might have very handsome Chairs *in the Way;* And thus, by Degrees, I found all my old Furniture stow'd up into the Garret, and every thing below alter'd for the better.

Had we stopp'd here, we might have done well enough; but my Wife being entertain'd with *Tea* by the Good Women she visited, we could do no less than the like when they visited us; and so we got a *Tea-Table* with all its Appurtenances of *China* and *Silver*. Then my Spouse unfortunately overwork'd herself in washing the House, so that we could do no longer without a *Maid*. Besides this, it happened frequently, that when I came home at *One,* the Dinner was but just put in the Pot; for, *My Dear thought really it had been but Eleven:* At other Times when I came at the same Hour, *She wondered I would stay so long, for Dinner was ready and had waited for me these two Hours.* These Irregularities, occasioned by mistaking the Time, convinced me, that it was absolutely necessary *to buy a Clock;* which my Spouse observ'd, *was a great Ornament to the Room!* And lastly, to my Grief, she was frequently troubled with some Ailment or other, and nothing did her so much Good as *Riding;* And *these Hackney Horses were such wretched ugly Creatures, that*—I bought a very fine pacing Mare, which cost £20. And hereabouts Affairs have stood for some Months past.

I could see all along, that this Way of Living was utterly inconsistent with my Circumstances, but had not Resolution enough to help it. Till lately, receiving a very servere Dun, which mention'd the next Court, I began in earnest to project Relief. Last Monday my Dear went over the River, to see a Relation, and stay a Fortnight, because *she could not bear the Heat of the Town.* In the Interim, I have taken my Turn to make Alterations, viz. I have turn'd away the Maid, Bag and Baggage (for what should we do with a Maid, who have (except my Boy) none but our selves). I have sold the fine Pacing Mare, and bought a good Milch Cow, with £3 of the Money. I have dispos'd of the Tea-Table, and put a Spinning

Wheel in its Place, which methinks *looks very pretty:* Nine empty Canisters I have stuff'd with Flax; and with some of the Money of the Tea-Furniture, I have bought a Set of Knitting-Needles; for to tell you a Truth, which I would have go no farther, *I begin to want Stockings.* The stately Clock I have transform'd into an Hour-Glass, by which I gain'd a good round Sum; and one of the Pieces of the old Looking-Glass, squar'd and fram'd, supplies the Place of the Great One, which I have convey'd into a Closet . . . because I know her Heart is set upon it. I will allow her when she comes in, to be taken suddenly ill with the *Headach,* the *Stomach-ach, Fainting Fits,* or whatever other Disorders she may think more proper; and she may retire to Bed as soon as she pleases: But if I do not find her in perfect Health both of Body and Mind the next Morning, away goes the aforesaid Great Glass, with several other Trinkets I have no Occasion for, to the Vendue that very Day. Which is the irrevocable Resolution of, Sir, Her loving Husband, and Your very humble Servant,

Anthony Afterwit

Postscript, You know we can return to our former Way of Living, when we please, if Dad will be at the Expence of it.

From Poor Richard's Almanack For . . . 1739:

Kind Reader,

ENcouraged by thy former Generosity, I once more present thee with an Almanack, which is the 7th of my Publication.—While thou are putting Pence in my Pocket, and furnishing my Cottage with Necessaries, *Poor Dick* is not unmindful to do something for thy Benefit. The Stars are watch'd as narrowly as old *Bess* watch'd her Daughter, and told a Tale of their Influences and Effects, which may do thee more good than a Dream of last Year's Snow.

Ingornat [*sic*] Men wonder how we Astrologers foretell the Weather so exactly, unless we deal with the old black Devil. Alas! 'tis as easy as pissing abed. For Instance; The Stargazer peeps at the Heavens thro' a long Glass: He sees perhaps TAURUS, or the great Bull, in a mighty Chase, stamping on the Floor of his House, swinging his Tail about, stretching out his Neck, and opening wide his Mouth. 'Tis natural from these Appearances to judge that this furious Bull is puffing, blowing, and roaring. Distance being consider'd, and Time allow'd for all this to come down, there you have Wind and Thunder. He spies perhaps VIRGO (or the Virgin) she turns her Head round as it were to see if any body observ'd her; then crouching down gently, with her Hands on her Knees, she looks wistfully for a while right forward. He judges rightly what she's about: And having calculated the Distance and allow'd Time for its Falling, finds that next Spring we shall have fine *April* shower.

· · ·

Some People observing the great Yearly demand for my Almanack, imagine I must by this Time have become rich, and consequently ought to call myself *Poor Dick* no longer. But, the Case is this, When I first begun to Publish, the Printer made a fair Agreement with me for my Copies, by Virtue of which he runs away with the greatest Part of the Profit. —However, much good may't do him; I do not grudge it him; he is a Man I have a great Regard for, and I wish his Profit ten times greater than it is. For I am, dear Reader, his, as well as thy

> *Affectionate Friend,*
> R. SAUNDERS

EXTRACTS FROM *The Drinkers Dictionary*[6]

B
He's Biggy
  Bewitch'd
  Block and Block
  Boozy
  Bowz'd

Been at Barbadoes
Piss'd in the Brook
His Head is full of Bees
Has drank more than he
  has bled
He's kiss'd black Betty

6. Labaree *et al.*, eds., *The Papers of Benjamin Franklin,* II (New Haven: Yale University Press, 1960), 173–78.

[201]

C
He's Cramp'd
   Wamble Crop'd
   Crack'd
   Half Way to Concord
   Loaded his Cart

D
He's Kill'd his Dog
   Took his Drops
   Dipp'd his Bill
   Seen the Devil

E
He's Enter'd
   Wet both Eyes
   Cock Eye'd
   Got the Pole Evil
   Got a Brass Eye
   Eat a Toad and half for
      Breakfast

F
He's Fishey
   Fox'd
   Fuddled
   Sore Footed
   Frozen
   Crump Footed
   Been to France
   Froze his Mouth
   His Flag is out
   Been at an Indian Feast

G
He's Groatable
   Been before George
   Had a Kick in the Guts
   Got the Gout
   Globular
   Got the Glanders

H
He's Half and Half
   Top Heavy
   Hiddey
   Loose in the Hilts
   Haunted with Evil Spirits

K
He's a King
   Seen the French King
   The King is his Cousin
   Got Kib'd Heels

L
He's in Liquor
   Lordly
   He makes Indentures
      with his Leggs

M
He sees two Moons
   Merry
   Middling
   Rais'd his Monuments

P
He drank till he gave up his
   Half-Penny
   Pidgeon Ey'd
   Pungey
   Priddy
   As good conditioned as a
      Puppy
   Has Scalt his Head Pan
   Been among the Philistines
   He's been among the
      Philippians

R
He's Rocky
   Raddled
   Rich
   Religious
   Lost his Rudder
   Been too free with Sir
      Richard
   Like a Rat in Trouble

S
He's Stitch'd
   Seafaring

In the Sudds
As Drunk as David's Sow
   Swampt
His Skin is full
He's burnt his Shoulder
He's got his Top Gallant
   Sails out
   Seen the Yellow Star
   Stiff as a Ring-bolt
   Half Seas over
   His Shoe pinches him
   He carries too much Sail
   Strubb'd
   Been too free with
      Sir John Strawberry
   Right before the
      Wind with all his
      Studding Sails out
   Has Sold his Senses

V
He makes Virginia
   Fence
Got the Indian Vapours

June 25, 1745

My dear Friend,

I know of no Medicine fit to diminish the violent natural Inclinations you mention; and if I did, I think I should not communicate it to you. Marriage is the proper Remedy. It is the most natural State of Man, and therefore the State in which you are most likely to find

[203]

solid Happiness. Your Reasons against entring into it at present, appear to me not well-founded. The circumstantial Advantages you have in View by postponing it, are not only uncertain, but they are small in comparison with that of the Thing itself, the being *married and settled*. It is the Man and Woman united that make the compleat human Being. Separate, she wants his Force of Body and Strength of Reason; he, her Softness, Sensibility and acute discernment. Together they are more likely to succeed in the World. A single Man has not nearly the Value he would have in that State of Union. He is an incomplete Animal. He resembles the odd Half of a Pair of Scissars. If you get a prudent healthy Wife, your Industry in your Profession, with her good Economy, will make a Fortune sufficient.

But if you will not take this Counsel, and persist in thinking a Commerce with the Sex inevitable, then I repeat my former Advice, that in all your Amours you should *prefer old Women to young ones*. You call this a Paradox, and demand my Reasons. They are these:

1. Because as they have more Knowledge of the World and their Minds are better stor'd with Observations, their Conversation is more improving and more lastingly agreable.

2. Because when Women cease to be handsome, they study to be good. To maintain their Influence over Men, they supply the Diminution of Beauty by an Augmentation of Utility. They learn to do a 1000 Services small and great, and are the most tender and useful of all Friends when you are sick. Thus they continue amiable. And hence there is hardly such a thing to be found as an old Woman who is not a good Woman.

3. Because there is no hazard of Children, which irregularly produc'd may be attended with much Inconvenience.

4. Because thro' more Experience, they are more prudent and discreet in conducting an Intrigue to prevent Suspicion. The Commerce with them is therefore safer with regard to your Reputation. And with regard to theirs, if the Affair should happen to be known, considerate People might be rather inclin'd to excuse an old Woman who would kindly take care of a young Man, form his

[204]

Manners by her good Counsels, and prevent his ruining his Health and Fortune among mercenary Prostitutes.

5. Because in every Animal that walks upright, the Deficiency of the Fluids that fill the Muscles appears first in the highest Part: The Face first grows lank and wrinkled; then the Neck; then the Breast and Arms; the lower Parts continuing to the last as plump as ever: So that covering all above with a Basket, and regarding only what is below the Girdle, it is impossible of two Women to know an old from a young one. And as in the dark all Cats are grey, the Pleasure of corporal Enjoyment with an old Woman is at least equal, and frequently superior, every Knack being by Practice capable of Improvement.

6. Because the Sin is less. The debauching a Virgin may be her Ruin, and make her for Life unhappy.

7. Because the Compunction is less. The having made a young Girl miserable may give you frequent bitter Reflections; none of which can attend the making an old Woman *happy*.

8. (thly and Lastly) They are *so grateful!!* Thus much for my Paradox. But still I advise you to marry directly; being sincerely

Your affectionate Friend.

Rules for Making Oneself a Disagreeable Companion[7]

RULES, by the Observation of which, a Man of Wit and Learning may nevertheless make himself a *disagreeable* Companion.

Your Business is to *shine;* therefore you must by all means prevent the shining of others, for their Brightness may make yours the less distinguish'd. To this End,

1. If possible engross the whole Discourse; and when other Matter fails, talk much of your-self, your Education, your Knowledge, your Circumstances, your Successes in Business, your Victories in Disputes, your own wise Sayings and Observations on particular Occasions, &c. &c. &c.

7. From *The Pennsylvania Gazette,* November 15, 1750.

2. If when you are out of Breath, one of the Company should seize the Opportunity of saying something; watch his Words, and, if possible, find somewhat either in his Sentiment of Expression, immediately to contradict and raise a Dispute upon. Rather than fail, criticise even his Grammar.

3. If another should be saying an indisputably good Thing; either give no Attention to it; or interrupt him; or draw away the Attention of others; or, if you can guess what he would be at, be quick and say it before him; or, if he gets it said, and you perceive the Company pleas'd with it, own it to be a good Thing, and withal remark that it had been said by Bacon, Locke, Bayle, or some other eminent Writer: thus you deprive him of the Reputation he might have gain'd by it, and gain some yourself, as you hereby show your great Reading and Memory.

4. When modest Men have been thus treated by you a few times, they will chuse ever after to be silent in your Company; then you may shine on without Fear of a Rival; rallying them at the same time for their Dullness, which will be to you a new Fund of Wit.

Thus you will be sure to please *yourself.* The polite Man aims at pleasing *others,* but you shall go beyond him even in that. A Man can be present only in one Company, but may at the same time be absent in twenty. He can please only where he *is,* you wherever you are *not.*

[206]

VIRGINIA SATIRE

AT MID-CENTURY

WE are indebted to Richard Beale Davis for the discovery and publication of a number of obscure manuscript satires written in mid-eighteenth-century Virginia.[1] According to his research, the two Irish or Scotch-Irish dialect letters included here were the work of a group of plantation "Gentlemen" in the Virginia House of Burgesses who took exception to the tax measures and war policies of Governor Robert Dinwiddie (1693-1770). From a variety of evidence, Professor Davis argues that these letters were written by one John Mercer of Marlboroughtown in Stafford—a planter whose quick pen and satiric wit earned him disbarment from the Virginia legal profession. Whether or not Mercer was the author, these letters represent one way in which isolated and often lonely planters filled the hours and communicated with one another.

Note should be taken of the degree to which satire, always a double-edged weapon, is turned against royal government and in favor of the settlers. The satirist presents himself in the guise of a frontier planter who is constantly vexed by the pretentious bungling of an inept and greedy tidewater aristocracy. Beginning with Alsop and running through Ebenezer Cook and Robert Hunter's *Androboros*, this democratic satire of British ineptitude in the wilderness was implied but overshadowed by the initially stronger desire to discredit new world barbarities. The early tendency was to ridicule the extent to which the colonists fell short of being English. The passage of time created an indigenous population who, through their longer exposure to the exigencies of North America, were

1. Richard Beale Davis, "The Colonial Virginia Satirist," *Transactions of the American Philosophical Society*, new series, 57, pt. 1, 1967.

[207]

inclined to turn the tables and notice how little English officials seemed to grasp the American situation.

In the two dialect satires which follow, the French-and-Indian War provided an appropriate context for an emerging American satire. The greater part of the fighting in that supremely important conflict took place in the interior, west of the Allegheny-Appalachian mountain chain, a wilderness little known to English imperial officials. As witnessed by the ill-fated Braddock expedition, the officers and strategies which emanated from the coastal settlements were too often as little sagacious as they were courageous. Among those in a position to know the realities of a largely Native American region, Williamsburg-based generals and tidewater-conceived battle-plans provided many an occasion for ridicule. Humor, in its indirect and masked fashion, was forging a weapon which, when wrenched from British hands, would cut in new and surprising directions.

W.H.K.

Virginia Purtomok river Jany
1756

Sir—I am serving my Country in a public Capacity, for I keeps a sti[ll] & stills whiskey wch. brings a grate deal of good Cumpany heer, only at firs [t ⟨?⟩] our Doctor grumbled because he said it had an Infernal perruma or some such a name; but now he corn drink it as fast as the best. & they likes it the better, were of they says it is almost as good as New England rum; & they duzzunt like to let it co[ol⟨?⟩], but takes it hot as it comes out—it would do you [r⟨?⟩] hart good to see what speseial copany they be halloring & hooping, & twenty or thurty talking together, so that you cant hear your own ears for them—& then they all gets to boxing, men, women & children, & knocking one another about, that to be sure nothing in Natare can be so diverting, tho'f I always minds that the women bears it the best—some o[f] 'um seems as tho'f they didnt desire

[208]

never to leave of, howsumdever, as soon as I think they have anuff, I calls for help & parts um . . . I hears sha [r⟨?⟩]p² is to rule the roast, over the Soljers in these parts, whereof I am very much disgruntled in behalf of the publick; for how shud he know how to mannige matters for us, that has no experience of our Countree affairs, that knows no more of makeing a Crap nor a new Negur? nor never purchased a hogshead of Tobacco in his life, nor never sold a Cargo, no nor never was a Store boy for if he had, we must acknowledge him to be a very fine Gentleman—nor never kept an Ordinary [tavern], nor was never an Under Sheriff, or any such creditable employment; why shd. Shirley³ put him so high in the Military. I suppose it is because he is just such a Coward as Shirley himself—that he is even afread that folks shud think he has any feer in him, which is worse nor to be afread of ones Shadow—for in that humor he may go & leed the pore men near the mouths of the great Guns, & so have a Chance to git some of them, & himself too plaguily hurted, nor I duzzent purceeve that he intends to make much of his bissyness as a Governor, which now a days when there is so much Cash a Sturring, must be allowd. to be as prittie a profitable sort of trade, well follored as any in the Countree; but I duzzent see why either he or Shirley, or any such desperados should command Armys, haddunt they better look . . . among the plantation Governors, (theres enouf of um) & pick out some staid elderly *Mon,* that has been bred up in the way of turning a penny the rite way, into his own pocket? . . . I wish I may die If I have not amind to acquaint his Majesty of all theese mismanagements—for its a shame so it is that the best of Kings shd. be the worst sarved . . .

Loving friend
Thomas BrownCoat

To Mr. Jonas Green at Annapolis

2. Horatio Sharpe (1718–1790), Governor of Maryland (1753–1769) who commanded an expedition against the French in 1754 before the arrival of the ill-fated General Braddock.

3. William Shirley (1694–1771), Governor of Massachusetts and Commander-in-Chief of the war effort after the death of Braddock.

From Timothy McOates To ——— Esqr., 3d May 1757

Dare Sur

Unkle Titus Oh! Grewell is after being dead, & I have got into his Royal Estate which I varily believes will be a vary Conshiderable Miss-Fortune to me, for the 5000 Aker tract was so pore dat I cud not parswade no boddy to pay me no Rents, & I was afread the land wd lie Idle—& I did hire won to go & be my tennant, & becaush he was my Cuntree man I was only to pay him five pounds Starling a Yeer for three livesh for his kindnesh—but as I was going on . . . in a prittie thriving way shom body came & told me that my tennant wd. not live upon de land any longer, becaush de Indian did kill him & since that time if I was to raise de Rent & give ten pounds a year I woudent get anodder tennant to stay dere for love nor moneys. & sho all de Quit rents, which I am afread will hardly find me shoose, which is but a sorry bargain indeed. I tink it looks almost as if I was chaited into an Estate, sho den I petishund our grate mens in town to grant me his Majestys most gracious writ of ay G—d Dammum—to maak sum body take it of my hands—but de laugh at me—& dey did say, dat de law had intail'd it sho fast—dat a tousand yoke of oxen & ten tousand lawyers wd. not hawl it away from me unless I wd. parswade de land to grow better—which I duz varily beleeve cannot be dun he ish so vary stony harted—dey says de McOates, is sarved well anuff,— becaush de McGruell was so wicked to taak up so much bad land, & dat since I did pay quit rents, it was a pitty but I wd. pay taxes too, sho you see dey is not without some sort of pitty—& dey says dat dey hopes dat de Indians will sarve Rejectments upon all de peeples on tudder side de blue Ridge—for dey says dey has no busyness dere. & dat de Dutch in particoller ought to have no sort of incurragement becaush de be too frugal & industrious & it will quite spoil de town & Cuntree by such abominable vices—& dat it is de better to shend for more Naigurs to seat de backlands becaush dere is no harm in 'um & wont tink of Stailing or cutting our T[hroa]ts, unless dey is advished to it by sum of de odder forreigners, & de says, de French & Indians did never tink of coming over de ridge

[210]

till shom of de Settlers in de new Cuntree did put it in to their heads
& show them de way, but now that de paths is grown up, it is
impossible dat de Indians will clime over such prodigious
Mountains—& dat if dey was to tempt it, dey wd. cartinly broak
deir neeks, or loose deir way, & perish in de woods, which dey is
quite Stranger too, —& did purchase de Indians of won
anudder—& dat their is now a bill preparing wch. when properly
passed into a law, shall oblige de Indians to stand to it whedder they
shall or not, & dat the asshemblee is actually Shitting a Tird—time
to Conshidder of ways & means to raise moneys to pay deir own
Shweet shelves, for having thus Brot owr affairs into a
Confushion—beshides, dey says de Indians have a more netural
love for us dan fur de French or for won anudder; & dat it dush not
stand for common sense & Raison that dey shud Reject our holy
Religions, & turn Idolaturs, which dey musht do if dey taaks to de
French who every buddy knows is all Rank papishes.

And our Grandees alsho says, let de matters happen never so
bad, dey has an Agent upon de stocks, who shall hire himshelf
vashtly Raisonable to go home. Just now & stay dere, & he after
spaaking good words for us to de besht of Kings, & to de besht of his
Ministers, & den we shall be all saafe anuff.

Dare Sur, I must needs tell you tho' that Titush before he did die,
[h]e was maake a will out of his own mouth, & did lave all his
parsonall Estate to your honour, but I could not find in my hart any
ting worth parting with but de little Book, which you is vary hartily
welcom to for fait now I doze tink dat shom of our Nobilitys wd.
contrive shome curshed Scheme or Charge upon it, if dey shd.
come acrossh it—ask fer de resht of Titushs Estate de sheep, & de
Oxen & Horses & Cash &c. I am advished by my Counsill Larned
in de Laws dat I had better stand shute—sho to let you see dat I
intends noting but dc fair ting—I intends to keep 'em, & prae dont
fail to shend me a Recait in full by de littell Naigur Boy, who is my
Returney in fact, in deshe shorts of Nagoshiashions.

Your loving friend

Occaquan   Timothy Mc Oates
3d May. 1757

[211]

PART FIVE

Satiric Invective
In the Revolution

INTRODUCTION

THE coming of the American War for Independence stimulated the flow of satiric wit from both patriot and tory presses. In the heat of growing crisis, two trends characterized the humor of the revolution: the tradition of satire was intensified as both sides presented themselves as the rightful spokesmen for tradition and sanity and ever more directly imputed wild and senseless innovations to the other. Secondly, as each event assumed cosmic proportions to those involved, humor became more narrowly focused on particular events and personalities.

The *Importer and the Indian,* for example, is based upon the efforts of Boston patriot leaders to persuade the merchants of other cities to enforce a strict nonimportation policy as a protest against British tax measures. While this policy was generally successful, New York merchants were somewhat less than rigid in its implementation and Boston-based propagandists periodically shamed them into their patriotic duty through satiric invective. In this case, at least, it is evident that the coming revolution signaled only a reaffirmation of the old prejudices against Native Americans.

The appeal to prejudice, a basic ingredient in fanning wartime hatreds, is further developed in *The Irishman's Epistle,* a celebration of the British defeat on the road from Concord to Boston, Massachusetts. As protest turned to fighting, satiric propaganda fanned all available sparks of anti-British resentment, finding, in this case, common ground between American and Irish independence movements. Despite the soundness of the trouncing administered to the redcoats on that April morning, it was then

[215]

unclear how the ensuing war would eventuate, and one senses that satire was an important tool in building patriot morale.

The Patriots of North-America issued from the press of James Rivington whose *Royal Gazette* became the bastion of Loyalist or Tory sympathies. Here, the recurrent British scorn for the empty ambitions of the provincials, a theme developed as early as 1708 by Ebenezer Cook, loses any politeness it once expressed and turns, instead, into overt loathing. This is worth noting. The revolution created few new directions in humorous writing, intensifying and clarifying the old themes instead. The conscious manipulation of events and personalities characteristic of comic writing is further suggested by the fact that Rivington, while publishing under the royal banner, became an American spy.[1]

The Expedition to Danbury expresses revolutionary hatred for those colonists who remained loyal to England. Incapable of seeing this preference in ideological or disinterested terms, rebel satirists imputed to them only the basest motives and characteristics. A shrill, hard laughter was the aim of patriot humorists who colored loyalists in treasonous hues.

By 1782, when the war for independence was nearing its conclusion, the British were portrayed in gore-drenched rapacity. The sacrifice of American life and the long, wearing attrition of war left little room for jocularity. The anonymous writer of the bogus letter, supposedly captured from a British-Seneca contingent, accuses the English with the most heinous, savage butchery. Satire has been transformed into a sharp-edged weapon with which revolutionary goals may be justified. The Native American serves, as always, as the foil in wartime imputations of the greater inhumanity.

In one sense, early American humor has come full circle: from the confidence-building invective of Nathaniel Ward to the nation-building accusations of wartime satire. As it always had, humor provided confidence and courage, for wilderness laughter was a necessary, functional ingredient in the lives of those who went before us.   W.H.K.

1. Catherine S. Crary, "The Tory and the Spy: The Double Life of James Rivington," *William and Mary Quarterly,* 3d. ser., XVI (1959), 61–72.

IMPORTERS AND INDIANS

THE MASSACHUSETTS SPY, August 25, 1770

From The Connecticut Courant.
Question.
WHAT is the difference betwixt an *Importer* and an *Indian?*
ANSWER 1. An Indian drinks Cyder—an Importer drinks the Blood of his Country.

2. An Indian is an Enemy only to himself—an Importer is an Enemy to America.

3. An Indian will sometimes fulfill his Engagements—but the strongest Cords, and the most solemn Engagements will not bind an Importer.

4. An Indian not having the Means of Light, is not subject to any tormenting Reflections—an Importer is eternally haunted with Apparitions, and the horror of a guilty Conscience.

5. An Importer, covered over with Tar, would shine with an artificial Lustre—whereas the black Colour of the Indian is natural.

6. How the Indian came *into* the Country is unknown—but if Importers should have their deserts, there would be no Witchcraft in determining how they would go *out*. From whence it appears that the State of an Indian is much better than that of an Importer.

THE IRISHMAN'S EPISTLE[1]

[1775]

The Epistle to the Troops in Boston
By my faith, but I think ye're all makers of bulls,
With your brains in your breeches, your guts in your skulls,
Get home with your muskets, and put up your swords,
And look in your books for the meaning of words.
You see now, my honies, how much your mistaken,
For Concord by discord can never be beaten.

How brave ye went out with your muskets all bright,
And thought to be-frighten the folks with the sight;
But when you got there how they powder'd your pums,
And all the way home how they pepper'd your bums,
And is it not, honeys, a comical crack,
To be proud in the face, and be shot in the back.

How come ye to think, now, they did not know how,
To be after their firelocks as smartly as you?
Why, you see now, my honies, 'tis nothing at all,
But to pull at the trigger, and pop goes the ball.

And what have you got now with all your designing,
But a town without victuals to sit down and dine in;

1. The Irishman's Epistle, *Pennsylvania Magazine,* I (May 1775), 232; reprinted in Frank Moore, *Songs and Ballads of the American Revolution* (New York: D. Appleton & Co., 1856), pp. 92–93.

And to look on the ground like a parcel of noodles,
And sing, how the Yankees have beaten the Doodles.
I'm sure if you're wise you'll make peace for a dinner,
For fighting and fasting will soon make ye thinner.

THE

PATRIOTS

OF

NORTH-AMERICA

Men plac'd, by Chance, or sov'reign Fate,
In Life's low, unambitious State;
Whilst undeprav'd, all amply share,
Wise, bounteous Nature's, equal Care.

To them, impartial Heav'n, assign'd,
Contentment calm, sweet Peace of Mind,
Deny'd them, Fame, and Pow'r, and Wealth,
But gave them, Temp-rance, Mirth, and Health;
Preserv'd them, from the fatal Snares,
Which Lux'ry spreads, for Fortune's Heirs.

From all the dire insidious Train,
Of wants unreal, Wishes vain,
Refinements false, and fierce Desires,
Voluptuous Arts, and lawless Fires;

Soft Blandishments, of Wealth, and Ease,
Which ruin, while they smile, and please
From childish, restless Whim, that reigns
In satiate Taste, and pamper'd Veins;
From the dire Weight, of vacant Time,
(That fatal Source of many a Crime;)

Envy of Pension, Power, and Place,
Vain Competition, sad Disgrace;
Honour, and Virtue, meanly sold
For Titles, Rank, or sordid Gold:
Corroding Cares, that constant wait
To check the Triumphs of the Great.

Doom'd them to earn, their wholesome Fare,
By gentler Toils, than anxious Care:
Free from the Woes, Ambition brings,
And made them, happier far, than Kings.

. . .

The Men deprav'd, who quit their Sphere,
Without Remorse, or Shame, or Fear,
And boldly rush, they know not where;
Seduc'd, alas! by fond Applause,
Of gaping Mobs, and loud Huzzas.
Unconscious all, of nobler Aim,
Than sordid Pelf, or vulgar Fame;
Men undefin'd, by any Rules,
Ambiguous Things, half Knaves, half Fools,
Whom God denied, the Talents great,
Requir'd, to make a Knave, complete;
Whom Nature form'd, vile Party-Tools,
Absurder much, than downright Fools,
Who from their own dear Puppet-Show,
The World's great Stage, pretend to know.
In Politics, mere Punchinellos,
Yet pass for rare, for clever Fellows;
Like Punch, who struts, and swears, and roars,
And calls his Betters, Rogues and Whores;
Like Punch, who speak their Prompter's Sense,

[221]

Like his, their pow'rful Eloquence,
Like his, their wond'ring Audience.
Poor, busy, factious, empty Things,
Who nothing know, of Courts or Kings;
Who Lords of Commons, ne'er have seen,
But think, they're like Committee-men;
By Rote, like clam-rous Parrots prate
Of Trade, Revenue, Church, and State.

.   .   .

In costive Brains, whole Weeks revolve,
To frame, some lawless, mad Resolve;
Some Hand-Bill vile, with Threatnings dire,
Of Murder, Feathers, Tar, or Fire,
Of rich, and poor, decide the Fate
With Scorn, of every Magistrate.

Is there among them, who can read,
It serves to turn, the Ideots Head;
Is there among them, who can write,
It serves to wreak the Miscreants Spite;
With Vipers leagu'd, in borrowed Name,
They hiss and blast their Neighbour's Fame:

.   .   .

Fair Truth, exclude from many a Press,
On Pain, of every dread Distress:
As Priests, their Flocks to circumvent,
Forbid, to read Christ's Testament,
With senseless Jargon, stupid Lies,
Like Morpheus,[1] close the People's Eyes,
Vile, false, pernicious Doctrines preach,
Rebellion rank, and Treason teach,

1. Greek God of Dreams.

[222]

Malignant o'er the Land they crawl,
And wither, blast, and poison all.

In Brothels, Corners, Fields, who lurk,
Fond of Cabals, detesting Work,
Neglect, their useful Occupations,
And starve themselves, to starve whole Nations. [2]
Whose foul, remorseless, guilty Souls,
Nor Laws of God, or Man, controuls;
Who scowl on Wealth, with envious Eye,
For Wealth, and Fame, and Influence sigh,
And strive intent, on Pelf, and Spoils,
To plunge the Land, in civil Broils.
Furious, and sleepless, till they see
One general, glorious Anarchy.
(Sad Scenes! where idle Ruffians gain
Riches unearn'd, by Toil or Pain,)
And ruthless, clear their bloody Way,
To wild, despotic, brutal Sway.
              . . .

Shall we applaud, this vagrant Crew,
Whose wretched Jargon, crude and new,
Whose Impudence, and lies delude
The harmless, ign'rant Multitude:
To Varlets, weak, impure, unjust,
The Reins, of Government, entrust.
Will Raggamuffins bold like these,
Protect our Freedom, Peace, or Ease?
Ah! surely no, it cannot be,
These are false Sons of Liberty.
              . . .

2. A reference to the pre-revolutionary nonimportation and embargo measures.

[223]

From Curio's frothy Declamation,
Decide on Trade, on Legislation,
On Charter Rights, and dread Taxation;
(That nauseous Cant, of old, and young,
That Theme, of every Booby's Tongue;)
Like Pettifoggers, pert, and raw,
Who grope, in Indexes for Law,
Prating of Books, they never read,
Toiling o'er Parchment, for their Bread;
Form'd at the most, to scrawl a Lease,
Yet dare to judge, of War, and Peace;
Whom, God for Scriv'ners only, meant,
Yet dare, to ape, high Parli'ment;
Scorning o'er mouldy Books to pore,
And learn, what pass'd, in Days of yore,
With wise, important Lessons, fraught,
How Patriots acted, Sages thought.

. . .

Men to Atlantic Empire born,
Look down on Greece, and Rome with Scorn:
Disdain their Maxims, Laws, or Rules,
To take from any States, or Schools,
Prefer their Mohawks, and their Creeks,
To Romans, Britons, Swiss, or Greeks,
Their nobler Souls, no Systems please,
But Savage Life, of Shawanese;[3]
Or Monsters fierce, of Woods and Seas.

. . .

With all this Bullying, Rant, and Noise,
They're giddy, thoughtless, helpless Boys;

3. Shawnee, a tribe of Indians living west of the Allegheny-Appalachian mountains.

[224]

Ah! cruel fate, alas! how soon,
Their idle, truant Race, is run.
Lo! Father comes, with wild Affright,
Their glorious Noon, is changed to Night:
Question'd poor Things, they cry and pray,
''Twas H—n—k, A—s, led the way.
'They call'd the Masters, Rogues and Fools,
'Swore 'twas a Shame, to be such Tools;
'That Ushers all, were hellish Imps,
'The Servants, Scoundrels, Rogues and Pimps!
'Combin'd, the Scholars to defraud,
'To pamper, cozen, wh—e, or baud;
'That Boys were all by Nature free,
'And College Laws, rank Slavery

.   .   .

'Let Fly in Master's Face, a F—t,
'And cried G—d d—n him, let's desert.'

Cowards when sober, bold when drunk,
At thoughts of Birch, their Spirits sunk,
Their Shillings, prodigally spent,
Conscious of Weakness, they relent;
Acknowledge, they have play'd the Fool,
Repent, return, are flogg'd in School;
And by their Suff'rings, wiser grown,
Their just Subordination own.
Some of the Lads, perchance have Sense,
Talents, and Wit, and Eloquence:
But want Experience, Practice, Knowledge,
And think the Cock-pit, Eton College.
Like them, the Men, whom Worlds unborn,
Shall name with horror, grief, and scorn;
Their mem'ries, and their Deeds detest,

[225]

Who robb'd a Land supremely blest,
Of sacred Rights, their Sires possest.
As savage fierce, as savage raw,
Averse from Order, Power and Law;
Less fit for Senates, than for Toys,
In politicks, at best but Boys.
Are these the Men, to bring Salvation,
To a distress'd, unhappy Nation;
Ah! surely no, it cannot be,
'Tis License, this, not Liberty.

THE EXPEDITION TO DANBURY

[1777]

IN April, 1777, a combined force of British troops and Tories sailed from New York to Connecticut aiming to destroy rebels' stores and supplies in Danbury. Led by Brigadier Generals Agnew and Sir William Erskine and Major-General William Tryon, this expedition fired the stores and beat back a counterattack led by the then patriot Benedict Arnold and Major General David Wooster. The use of tories as well as the burning of private property enraged the rebel press and produced the following satire.

W.H.K.

THE EXPEDITION TO DANBURY[1]

Scene—New York

Without wit, without wisdom, half-stupid and drunk,
And rolling along arm in arm with his punk,
The gallant Sir William,[2] who fights all by proxy,
Thus spoke to his soldiers, held up by his doxy:

'My boys, I'm a going to send you with Tryon,[3]
To a place where you'll all get as groggy as I am;

---

1. Pennsylvania *Gazette,* May 14, 1777; reprinted in Moore, *Diary of the American Revolution,* I (New York: Charles T. Evans, 1863), 428–32.
2. Sir William Howe, commander of British forces and a reputed heavy drinker and womanizer.
3. A Tory and ex-governor of New York and North Carolina.

And the wounded, when well, shall receive a full gill,
But the slain be allowed just as much as they will.
By a Tory from Danbury, I've just been informed,
That there's *nobody there, so the place shall be storm'd.'*

Tryon

If there's nobody *there,* sir, and nobody *near it,*
Two thousand will conquer the whole, never fear it.

(Joe Gallop-away,[4] a refugee Tory, with Several others.)

Joe

Good soldiers, go fight, that we all may get rich.

Soldiers

Go get you a halter. * * * *
Get out, and go live in the woods upon nuts,
Or I'll give you my bayonet plump in your guts
D'ye think you contemptible thief-looking crew,
That we fight to get beef for such rascals as you?

Tryon

Come on, my brave boys, now as bold as a lion,
And march for the honor of General Tryon;
My lads, there's no danger, for this you may know,
That I'd let it alone if I thought it was so.

Scene—Connecticut. Troops Landed.

4. Prominent loyalist and author of a rejected plan for reconciliation between Britain and the colonies, Joseph Galloway.

Tryon

In cunning and canting, deceit and disguise,
In cheating a friend, and inventing of lies,
I think I'm a match for the best of my species,
But in this undertaking I feel all in pieces;
So I'll fall in the rear, for I'd rather go last;—
Come, march on, my boys, let me see you all past;
For his Majesty's service (so says my commission)
Requires that I *bring up* the whole expedition.

Scene—Danbury. Troops Arrived.

Tryon

Come, Halloo, my lads, for the day is our own,
No rebels are here; not a soul in the town;
So fire all the houses, and when in a blaze,
We'll honor the King with a shout of huzzas.

(A noise among the soldiers)

Tryon

In his Majesty's name, what's this mutinous jargon?

Soldiers

We came to get drunk, sir, for that was the bargain!

Irish Soldier, Drunk

Huzza for the Congress—the Congress and toddy.

Tryon

You scoundrel, I'll run you quite through the body.

[229]

Second Irish Soldier

By the head of St. Paddy,
I care not a louse for King George nor his daddy.

Third Irish Soldier

What plenty is here! Oh what eating and drinking!
Who'd stay in New York, to be starving and—.

Fourth Irish Soldier

The rebels, huzza! in a hat full of rum.

Fifth Irish Soldier

Come let us drink bumpers,[5] Jack,—out of a drum.

Scotch Soldier

Laird Bute[6] and his clan are a bundle of thieves.

English Soldier

Lord North[7] and his gang are a kennel of slaves.

Welsh Soldier

And a Welshman, prave poys, never harbors with knaves.

5. Large goblets.
6. John Stuart, Earl of Bute, a Scot, tutor to George III and his prime minister from 1761–1763.
7. Frederick, Lord North, prime minister from 1770 to 1782, who presided over the loss of the colonies.

All

Then let us go over,
Who'd stay to be starved, that might thus live in clover?

(They Sing)

Let freedom and love be the glee of our song,
Let America flourish—the Congress grow strong,
And brave Washington *conqueror* all the day long.

(A consulation of officers. At a distance, houses and stores on fire.)

Tryon

I wish I was back, for I'm woefully scar'd,
The light will be seen and the noise will be heard,
And the rebels will gather so thick in our way,
That whether we run for it or whether we stay,
The fate of the whole will be doubtful—and then—

(A sudden alarm; an officer in a fright gallops about crying)

To arms, to arms, to arms—ten thousand men
Are pouring from the clouds—ten thousand more
Are got between the army and the shore,
Ten thousand women too.

Tryon

Run, run; stop, stop,
Here, help me on my horse before I drop.

(Enter an officer from New York. To Tryon.)

The King hath promised, sir, you shall be *knighted*.

[231]

Tyron

The devil take the King—for I am so frighted—

Officer

But, sir, you must attend to what I've said.

Tryon

Why, then, the King must knight me when I'm dead.

Officer

But I bring orders, sir, which say *'you must'*—

Tryon

Aye, *must* or *not,* I'll have a gallop first. (*Sets off with the whole after him.*)

Scene—The Shipping

(*Troops on board.* Tryon *surrounded with Surgeons*)

Tryon

My belly's full of balls—I hear them rattle.

Surgeon

'Tis only, sir, the echo of the battle.

Tryon

Do search me over—see where 'tis I'm wounded.

Surgeon

You are not hurt, sir.

Tryon

Then I am confounded;
For as I stood, not knowing what to do,
Whether to fight, to fly, or to pursue,
A cannon ball, of two and thirty pound,
Struck me just where Sir Peter[8] got his wound;
Then passing on between my horse's ears—

Surgeon

Compose yourself, good sir—forget your cares,
You are not slain—you are alive and well.

Tryon

Between my horse's ears, and down he fell,
Then getting up again,

Surgeon

Dear Sir, compose,
And try to get yourself into a doze;
The hurt you've got is not so dangerous deep,
But bleeding, shaving, patience, time, and sleep,
With blisters, clysters, physic, air, and diet,
Will set you up again, if you'll be quiet.

Tryon

So thick, so fast, the balls and bullets flew,
Some hit me here, some there, some thro' and thro'—
And so by thousands did the rebels muster
Under Generals Arnold and old Wooster,
That let me, let me, let me, let me but
Get off alive—*farewell Connecticut.*

8. Commodore Sir Peter Parker who led a naval bombardment of Sullivan's Island during which he received wounds to his posterior.

[233]

CAPTAIN GERRISH'S LETTER

[1782]

EXTRACT of a Letter from Capt. Gerrish, of the New-England Militia, Dated Albany, March 7 (1782)[1]

The Peltry taken in the Expedition . . . will as you see amount to a good deal of Money. The Possession of this Booty at first gave us Pleasure; but we were struck with Horror to find among the Packages, 8 large ones containing SCALPS of our unhappy Country-folks, taken in the three last Years by the Senneka Indians from the Inhabitants of the Frontiers of New-York, New-Jersey, Pennsylvania, and Virginia, and sent by them as a Present to Col. Haldimend, Governor of Canada, in order to be by him transmitted to England. They were accompanied by the following Letter to that Gentleman.

Teoga, Jan. 3d, 1782.

May it please your Excellency,

'At the Request of the Senneka Chiefs I send herewith to your Excellency, under the care of James Boyd, eight Packs of Scalps, cured, dried, hooped and painted, with all the Indian triumphal Marks, of which the following is Invoice and Explanation.

No. I. Containing 43 Scalps of Congress Soldiers killed in different Skirmishes; these are stretched on black Hoops, 4 Inches diameter; the inside of the Skin painted Red, with a small black Spot to note their being killed with Bullets. Also 62 of Farmers, killed in their Houses; the Hoops red the Skin painted brown, and marked with a Hoe; a black circle all round, to denote their being surprised in the Night; and a black Hatchet in the middle, signifying their being killed with that Weapon.

1. "Supplement" to the Boston *Independent Chronicle*, February 28, 1782.

No 4. Containing 102 of Farmers, mixed of the several Marks above; only 18 marked with a little yellow Flame, to denote their being of Prisoners burnt alive, after being scalped, their Nails pulled out by the Roots, and other Torments: one of these latter supposed to be of a rebel Clergyman, his Band being fix'd to the Hoop of his Scalp. . . .

No. 5. Containing 88 Scalps of Women; Hair long, braided in the indian Fashion, to shew they were Mothers; Hoops blue; Skin yellow Ground, with little red Tadpoles to represent, by way of Triumph, the Tears of Grief occasioned to their Relations; . . .

No. 8. This package is a Mixture of all the Varieties abovementioned, to the Number of 123 with a Box of Birch Bark, containing 29 little Infants' scalps of various Sizes; small white Hoops; white Ground; no Tears; and only a little black Knife in the Middle, to shew they were ript out of their Mothers' bellies. . . .

I doubt not but that your Excellency will think it proper to give some farther Encouragement to those People . . .

Your Excellency's most obedient
And most humble Servant,
JAMES CRAUFURD

It was at first proposed to bury these scalps; but Lieutenant Fitzgerald, who you know has got Leave of Absence to go for Ireland on his private Affairs, said he thought it better they should proceed to their Destination; and if they were given to him, he would undertake to carry them to England, and hang them all up in some dark night on the Trees in St. James's Park, where they could be seen from the King and Queen's Palaces in the Morning; for that the Sight of them might perhaps strike Muley Ishmael (as he called him) with some Compunction of Conscience. They were accordingly delivered . . . To-morrow they go with the Baggage in a Waggon for Boston, and will probably be there in a few days after this Letter.

I am, &c.
SAMUEL GERRISH
Boston, March 20.

[235]

Monday last arrived here Lieutenant Fitzgerald above mentioned, and Yesterday the Waggon with the Scalps. Thousands of People are flocking to see them this Morning, and all Mouths are full of Execrations. Fixing them to the Trees is not approved. It is now proposed to make them up in decent little Packets, seal and direct them; one to the King, containing a Sample of every Sort for his Museum; one to the Queen . . . the Rest to be distributed among both Houses of Parliament; a double Quantity to the Bishops.